教育部基础学科拔尖学生培养计划 2.0 项目(20212060)
EFL Learning Series for Top-notch Innovative Talents
拔尖创新人才英语系列教材

U0949688

生 存 口 语

Survival Oral English

丛书主编　周小兰
主　　编　左　宁　周小兰
副 主 编　宁　明　庄新红　甲鲁海
　　　　　王　静　孙路平
编　　者　李钧秀　薛冠琳　董艳灵

山东大学出版社
SHANDONG UNIVERSITY PRESS
·济南·

图书在版编目(CIP)数据

生存口语:汉、英 / 左宁,周小兰主编. —济南:山东大学出版社,2021.12(2024.1 重印)
ISBN 978-7-5607-7268-4

Ⅰ. ①生… Ⅱ. ①左… ②周… Ⅲ. ①英语—口语—自学参考资料 Ⅳ. ①H319.9

中国版本图书馆 CIP 数据核字(2021)第 250469 号

责任编辑 孙艳凤
封面设计 牛 钧

出版发行 山东大学出版社
社 址 山东省济南市山大南路 20 号
邮政编码 250100
发行热线 (0531)88363008
经 销 新华书店
印 刷 济南新科印务有限公司
规 格 787 毫米×1092 毫米 1/16
14.75 印张 337 千字
版 次 2021 年 12 月第 1 版
印 次 2024 年 1 月第 3 次印刷
定 价 48.00 元

版权所有 侵权必究

Contents

Unit 1 Health

Part A Ailments and Illnesses

A1. Introduction

Physical Signs That You Shouldn't Ignore

You sleep poorly.

The stress hormone cortisol is supposed to drop at night, allowing your body to rest and recharge. When you suffer from insomnia, it's often because your cortisol levels are revved up at night as a result of too many "fight-or-flight" stress responses in your body. When your stress response is turned on, your body's natural self-repair mechanisms get flipped off. Then BINGO. You get sick.

You're getting shorter.

Strange. The doctor just measured you two years ago. You used to be 5 feet and 7 inches. Now you're 5 feet and 6.5 inches. Why are you shrinking? It's probably because your bones are starting to degenerate as a result of osteoporosis. Aging doesn't have to mean bone loss. It's possible to have healthy bones your whole life, so if you're losing stature, it's worth noting.

To protect your bones, make sure you're getting enough natural calcium, vitamin D, weight bearing exercise, and — the one most doctors won't prescribe — relaxation responses, which can help your bones strengthen themselves.

You're "apple-shaped".

If your body has extra weight around the waist and belly (aka visceral fat), this is sometimes referred to as "apple-shaped". Apple-shaped individuals — particularly those who have a waist circumference greater than 35 — may be at a higher risk of metabolic disease.

You're always tired.

Sure, your fatigue might be the result of burning the midnight oil and then getting up early for CrossFit or child care. You could be tired because your thyroid isn't functioning properly, your adrenal glands are burned out, or your body is exhausted from expending all your resources trying to protect you from the toxic overload you're bombarding your system with because of processed foods, cigarettes, alcohol, or environmental exposures.

Even more commonly, you could be wiped out because your stress responses are flipped on all the time — and your self-repair mechanisms are in overdrive, trying to protect you from infection, cancer, and a whole host of other serious illnesses. Sometimes chronic fatigue is the only symptom that your nervous system is stuck in chronic, repetitive stress response — the whisper that precedes your body's rebel yell. So don't dismiss exhaustion.

Your urine is dark yellow.

Hydration is essential to maintaining a healthy body, and when you're well hydrated, your urine should be almost completely clear. If you peer into the toilet and see a lot of yellow, you're probably not drinking enough fluids. Remember, caffeinated or alcoholic beverages are dehydrating, not hydrating, so stick to water, herbal or green tea, coconut water, or green juice.

You snore.

Snoring may be the only early sign of sleep apnea, a sleep disorder characterized by obstruction in the airways that can increase your risk of pulmonary hypertension and subsequent heart failure.

You're always anxious.

You might think anxiety is all in your head — and it certainly can be. Anxiety can start as a feeling in your mind that translates into the physiology of your body and predisposes you to diseases. But sometimes, anxiety can go the other way. Anxious feelings can result from hormone imbalances, hyperthyroidism, and more.

Not sure what's causing your anxiety? Start by asking your inner wisdom what is causing you to feel anxious. Usually, anxiety is the result of areas of your life being out of alignment with your true self. If you feel anxious for no reason at all, ask your doctor to test your hormones.

You only move your bowels once a day — or even every other day.

Healthy bowels move every time you eat a meal. It's called the "gastro colic reflex". When you insert food into the digestive tract, healthy bowels move to eliminate waste and make room for new nutrition. Otherwise, you wind up, well, full of you-know-what. When you're constipated, toxins in the body can seep through the lining of the bowel, enter the bloodstream, and cause inflammation, which can put you at risk of a whole host of body-yelling health conditions. Your potty is your friend, my dear!

You catch every cold and flu.

We're all exposed to viruses and bacteria every day, but a healthy individual should be able to fight off these pathogens the majority of the time. If you're that person who catches every cold your friends have or gets sick every time your kids do, your immune system may not be functioning optimally. This can not only put you at risk of infectious diseases, but also other long-term health issues.

Your lips crack, especially at the corners of your mouth.

Cracked lips, also known as "cheilitis", can signal a deficiency in B vitamins, especially vitamin B12, which can put you at risk of illnesses like anemia. For a simple source of B12, mix up my favorite go-to snack — popcorn, olive oil, nutritional yeast, truffle salt, and cayenne pepper. (It's the nutritional yeast that is a potent source of B12.)

Your skin is always breaking out.

If you have frequent outbreaks of acne, psoriasis, eczema, or other rashes, your health may be on the fritz. Your skin is the body's largest organ of elimination, and if it's acting up, your body may be trying to tell you something. Your skin may signal food or other allergies, but your skin is also very often a sign that your nervous system is in stress response.

While all of these signs may sound a bit concerning, just remember you can always take action to protect your overall health and well-being.

(Adapted from *mindbodygreen.com*)

A2. Words and Expressions

Vocabulary

1. asthma /ˈæzmə/ *n.* 气喘，哮喘
2. influenza /ˌɪnfluˈenzə/ *n.* (flu 的正式说法)流行性感冒，流感
3. measles /ˈmiːzlz/ *n.* 麻疹，风疹
4. mumps /mʌmps/ *n.* 流行性腮腺炎
5. diabetes /ˌdaɪəˈbiːtiːs/ *n.* 糖尿病
6. hyperlipemia /ˌhaɪpəlɪˈpiːmɪə/ *n.* 高血脂症
7. hyperglycemia /ˌhaɪpəglaɪˈsiːmɪə/ *n.* 高血糖症

Medical Emergency	**急症**
in shock	休克
in coma / be unconscious	昏迷
heatstroke	中暑
frostbite	冻伤
heart attack	心脏病发作
asthma attack	哮喘发作
allergic reaction	过敏反应
swallow poison	吞服毒药
food poisoning	食物中毒
overdose on drugs	服药过量
get an electric shock	触电
palpitation	心悸
respiratory arrest	呼吸骤停
stroke	中风
epilepsy	癫痫

Illnesses	**疾病**
the flu / influenza	流行性感冒，流感
strep throat	脓毒性咽喉炎
measles	麻疹，风疹
mumps	腮腺炎
chicken pox	水痘

athlete foot	足癣
cancer	癌症
depression	抑郁症
diabetes	糖尿病
pneumonia	肺炎
heart disease	心脏病
kidney stone	肾结石
high blood pressure / hypertension	高血压
high blood fat / hyperlipemia	高血脂
high blood sugar / hyperglycemia	高血糖
anorexia nervosa	神经性厌食症
thyroid nodule	甲状腺结节
fatty liver	脂肪肝

Vocabulary

1. migraine/ˈmiːɡreɪn/ *n*. 偏头痛
2. toothache /ˈtuːθeɪk/ *n*. 牙痛
3. congest /kənˈdʒest/ *v*. (使)充满,(使)挤满,(使)拥堵
4. stuffed /stʌft/ *adj*. 堵塞的,塞满的
5. laryngitis /ˌlærɪnˈdʒaɪtɪs/ *n*. 喉炎
6. tonsillitis /ˌtɒnsəˈlaɪtɪs/ *n*. 扁桃体炎
7. arthritis /ɑːˈθraɪtɪs/ *n*. 关节炎

Ailments	**小病**
headache	头痛
migraine	偏头痛
earache	耳痛
backache	背痛
toothache	牙痛
stomachache	胃痛
sore throat	咽喉痛
fever/temperature	发烧
cold	感冒

infection	感染
rash	皮疹(皮肤)
insect bite	蚊虫叮咬
sunburn	晒伤
stiff neck	落枕
runny nose	流鼻涕
congested / blocked / stuffed nose	鼻塞
bloody nose / nosebleed	流鼻血
blister	水泡
wart	疣
laryngitis	喉炎
tonsillitis	扁桃体炎
arthritis	关节炎
an ear infection	耳部感染
canker sore	口疮;口腔溃疡
dry eye syndrome	干眼症

Vocabulary

1. sprain /spreɪn/ *v.* 扭伤(关节)
2. bruise /bruːz/ *v.* 碰伤,瘀伤
3. swollen /ˈswoʊlən/ *adj.* 肿大的,膨胀的,大于正常的

Injuries	**受伤**
bleed	流血
twist / sprain	扭伤(关节)
scratch	抓伤
scrape	擦伤
burn	烧伤
scald	烫伤
hurt	受伤
bruise	瘀伤
cut	切破,割破
dislocate	脱臼

break	骨折
swollen	肿大的，肿胀的

Vocabulary

1. hiccup /ˈhɪkʌp/ *n*. 打嗝
2. diarrhea /ˌdaɪəˈrɪə/ *n*. 腹泻
3. nauseous /ˈnɑːʃəs/ *adj*. 感到恶心的，想呕吐的
4. indigestion /ˌɪndɪˈdʒestʃən/ *n*. 消化不良
5. shiver /ˈʃɪvə/ *v*. (因寒冷、疾病或恐惧而)轻微颤抖，发抖

Symptoms	**症状**
acne / pimples / zit	粉刺，青春痘
hiccup / burp / belch	打嗝
chill	寒战
sweat / perspire	流汗
heat rash	痱子(皮肤)
itchy	痒的
painful	疼痛的
cramp	抽筋，痉挛，(胃部)绞痛
diarrhea	腹泻，痢疾
chest pain	胸痛
chest infection	胸腔感染
ear infection	耳部感染
shortness of breath	呼吸短促
blush / flush	脸红，面部泛起的红晕
faint	昏厥
dizzy	晕眩
lightheaded	头晕
nauseous	感到恶心的，想呕吐的
vomit / throw up	呕吐
bloated	胃胀的，饮食过度的
exhausted	筋疲力尽的
excessive fatigue	过劳，极度疲倦

congested	充血的
cough	咳嗽
sneeze	打喷嚏
snore	打鼾
wheeze	气喘
constipation	便秘
have piles	长痔疮
shiver	轻颤,发抖(因寒冷、疾病或恐惧等)
body odor	体臭
venous swelling	静脉肿胀
choke	窒息,哽咽

Vocabulary

1. adhesive /əd'hiːsɪv/ *adj*. 黏着的,有黏性的
2. antiseptic /ˌæntɪ'septɪk/ *adj*. 不受感染的,消过毒的,无菌的
3. sterile /'sterəl/ *adj*. (生物)不育的,(土地)贫瘠的,不长作物的
4. hydrogen /'haɪdrədʒən/ *n*. 氢,氢气
5. gauze /gɑːz/ *n*. (包扎伤口或过滤用的)纱布
6. antihistamine /ˌæntɪ'hɪstəmɪn/ *n*. (治疗过敏症的)抗组(织)胺剂,抗组(织)胺药
7. aspirin /'æsprɪn/ *n*. 阿司匹林(尤用于治疗头疼、发烧和炎肿)
8. Heimlich /'haɪmlɪk/ *n*. (美)海姆利克氏操作法
9. tourniquet /'tɜːnɪkɪt/ *n*. 止血带

First Aid	**急救**
first-aid kit	急救箱
adhesive bandage / band-aid	创可贴
antiseptic cleaning wipe	消毒纸巾
sterile dressing pad	无菌敷料垫
hydrogen peroxide	过氧化氢
antibiotic ointment	抗生素药膏
gauze	(包扎伤口或过滤用的)纱布
adhesive tape	胶布

tweezer	镊子
ice pack	冰袋
antihistamine cream	抗组胺剂
elastic bandage / ace bandage	弹力绷带
aspirin	阿司匹林
painkiller	止痛药
cardiopulmonary resuscitation (CPR)	心肺复苏术
have no pulse	没有脉搏
rescue breathing	人工呼吸
the Heimlich maneuver	海姆利克急救法
splint	用夹板固定
tourniquet	止血带

Vocabulary

1. thermometer /θəˈmɔːmɪtə/ *n.* 温度计,体温计
2. gauge /geɪdʒ/ *n.* 测量仪器,计量器
3. syringe /səˈrɪndʒ/ *n.* 注射器,注射筒
4. stethoscope /ˈsteθəskoʊp/ *n.* 听诊器
5. intimidating /ˌɪnˈtɪmədeɪtɪŋ/ *adj.* 令人紧张的,吓人的
6. daunting /ˈdɑːntɪŋ/ *adj.* 令人发怵的

Medical Examination	**体检**
have / get a medical examination	进行体检
go for an annual physical exam	进行每年一度的体检
have regular check-ups	进行常规或定期体检
schedule an appointment	预约
receive an in-depth diagnosis	接受深入的诊断
assess the overall wellness	评估整体健康状况
reduce the risk of developing a disease	降低患病的风险
disease screening	疾病筛查
detect early signs	发现早期征兆
take precautionary steps	采取预防措施
contract a disease	患上疾病

adjust one's lifestyle	调整生活方式
use a scale to measure one's height and weight	用秤测量身高和体重
use a thermometer to take one's temperature	用体温计量体温
use a blood pressure gauge to check one's blood pressure	用血压计测量血压
use a needle / syringe to draw one's blood	用注射器抽血
use an eye chart to examine one's eyes	用视力表检查眼睛
use a stethoscope to listen to one's heartbeat	用听诊器来听心跳
use an X-ray machine to take a chest X-ray	用X光机做胸部X光检查
cause discomfort	引起不适
intimidating	令人紧张的，吓人的
daunting	令人发怵的

Vocabulary

1. intravenous /ˌɪntrəˈviːnəs/ *adj*. 进入静脉的(缩写为 I.V.)
2. hypodermic /ˌhaɪpoʊˈdərːmɪk/ *adj*. 皮下注射的
3. shot /ʃɑːt/ *n*. (药品或毒品的)一次注射量
4. lozenge /ˈlɑːzəndʒ/ *n*. 润喉糖，润喉含片
5. acupuncture /ˈækjəpʌŋktʃə/ *n*. 针刺疗法
6. decongestant /ˌdiːkənˈdʒestənt/ *n*. 减充血剂
7. capsule /ˈkæpsəl/ *n*. 胶囊

Medical Treatment and Advice	**治疗与建议**
intravenous injection / drip	静脉注射
intramuscular injection	肌肉注射
hypodermic injection	皮下注射
have an injection / get a shot	打针
give someone an injection	给某人打针
give someone a shot of...	给某人注射一剂……
crutch	腋杖
cane	手杖
walker	(老年或小孩等用的)学步车，助行架
wheelchair	轮椅
physical therapy	物理疗法
prescription	处方，药方

sling	(悬吊受伤手臂的)悬带,吊腕带
cast	石膏绷带,石膏夹
brace	腿部规形夹
drink fluids	补水
vitamin	维生素
cold tablet	感冒药
cough syrup	止咳糖浆
throat lozenge	润喉糖,润喉含片
get acupuncture	针灸治疗,施行针刺疗法
clean and dress the wound	清洗并包扎伤口
close the wound	缝合伤口
antacid	抗酸剂
decongestant spray / nasal spray	喷鼻剂,鼻腔喷雾剂
eye drops	眼药水
ointment	药膏,软膏
cream	乳膏
lotion	乳液
over-the-counter (OTC) medicine	非处方药
prescription medicine	处方药
take a pill / tablet / capsule	吃药丸/药片/胶囊
caplet	囊片(椭圆胶囊形糖衣药片)
teaspoon	一茶勺的量
tablespoon	一汤勺的量
heating pad	电热垫
air humidifier	空气加湿器
surgery	外科手术
minimally invasive surgery	微创手术

A3. Situational Conversations

Conversation 1 Talking about Stomachache

P: Patient D: Doctor

P: I've had a stomachache and **loose motions** since last night. I also vomited a few times in the night.

D: What did you eat yesterday?

P: I ate some snacks at the **roadside eatery**. It's likely a result of that.

D: Likely you ate **contaminated food**. Because of diarrhea, you've lost plenty of body fluids. You need to be **hydrated.** Drink water regularly. Mix some Glucon-D powder or Electoral in it. Fruit juice is fine too. Avoid caffeine, dairy products, and solid foods at least till evening. And get plenty of rest.

P: Any medicines, doctor?

D: Yes, I'm **prescribing** a few to control diarrhea.

P: Thank you, doctor.

(Adapted from *lemongrad.com*)

☞**Notes**

- **loose motions**: the condition of having three or more loose or liquid bowel movements in a day. It is a common cause of death in developing countries and the second most common reason for infant deaths worldwide. The loss of fluids during loose motions can cause dehydration and electrolyte disturbances.
- **roadside eatery**: an informal way to describe a restaurant or café which is located at the roadside with a lack of sanitation.
- **contaminated food**: polluted or poisonous food, which may cause people's sickness. It might be contaminated by dirt, chemicals and radiation.
- **hydrated**: having absorbed enough water or other liquid.
- **prescribe**: (of a doctor) to say what medical treatment someone should have.

Conversation 2　Having a Physical Examination

P: **Patient**　**D**: **Doctor**

D: When did you last come in for a physical exam?

P: I had my last physical exam two years ago.

D: Have you had any other exams recently? Blood work, an **EKG** or an **ultrasound**?

P: Well, I had a few X-rays at the dentist.

D: How have you been feeling in general?

P: Pretty well. No complaints, really.

D: Could you roll up your left sleeve? I'd like to take your blood pressure.

P: Certainly.

D: 120 over 80. That's fine. You don't seem to be overweight, that's good. Do you exercise regularly?

P: No, not really. If I run up a flight of stairs, it takes me a while to get my breath back. I need to get out more.

D: That would be a good idea. How about your diet?

P: I think I have a pretty balanced diet. You know, I'll have a hamburger from time to time, but generally, I have well-balanced meals.

D: That's good. Now, I'm going to listen to your heart.

P: Ooh, that's cold!

D: Don't worry; it's just my **stethoscope**. Now, breathe in and hold your breath. Please pull up your shirt, and breathe deeply... Everything sounds good. Let's take a look at your throat. Please open wide and say "ah".

P: "Ah".

D: OK. **Everything looks ship shape.** I'm going to order some blood work and that's about it. Take this slip to the front desk and they'll arrange an appointment for the tests.

P: Thank you, doctor. Have a nice day.

(Adapted from *thoughtco.com*)

☞ **Notes**

- **EKG**: the abbreviation for electrocardiogram, which is a drawing or electronic image made by an electrocardiograph.
- **ultrasound**: a type of imaging test to examine the internal organs using very high-frequency sound waves.
- **stethoscope**: a piece of medical equipment that doctors use to listen to your heart and lungs.
- **"Everything looks ship shape."**: something that is neat and with everything in its correct place. Its adjective form is shipshape.

Conversation 3 Getting a Prescription from the Doctor

P: **Patient** **D**: **Doctor**

P: ... what about the problems I've been having in sleeping?

D: I'm going to give you a **prescription** for some medicine to help you get a better night's sleep.

P: Thank you, doctor.

D: Here, you can get this prescription at any **pharmacy**.

P: How often should I take the medicine?

D: Just take one pill about 30 minutes before you go to bed.

P: How long should I take them?

D: The prescription is for thirty days. If you're not sleeping well after thirty days, I'd like you to come back in.

P: Is there anything else I can do to help me sleep at night?

D: Don't worry so much about things at work. I know, I know... easier said than done.

P: Should I stay home from work?

D: No, I don't think that's necessary. Just remember to stay calm.

(Adapted from *thoughtco.com*)

☞**Prescriptions include**:

- patient identifier: first and last name of the patient, as well as the date of birth (DOB).
- medication (also named "drug"): the medicine that is prescribed.
- strength: how strong the medication prescribed is (50 mg, 100 mg, etc.).
- amount: how much the patient should take each dose.
- frequency: how often the patient should take the medicine.
- route: how the patient should take the medicine (by mouth, **topical**, **sublingual**, etc.).
- refills: how often the prescription should be renewed.
- signature: signature of the **physician** written in the prescription.
- date: the day on which the prescription was written.

☞**Notes**

- **prescription**: a piece of paper on which a doctor writes the details of the medicine or drugs that someone needs.
- **pharmacy**: a licensed store in which medicines are prepared and sold.
- **topical**: a topical medical product is used on the outside of the body or skin.
- **sublingual**: under the tongue.
- **physician**: a medical doctor, especially one who has general skills and is not a surgeon.

A4. Picture Knowledge

Pic. 1-1 My body

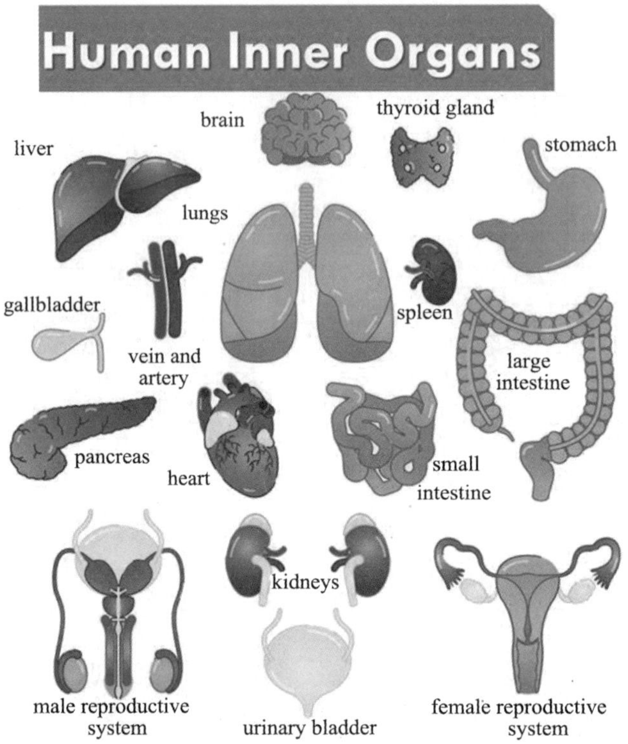

Pic. 1-2 Human inner organs

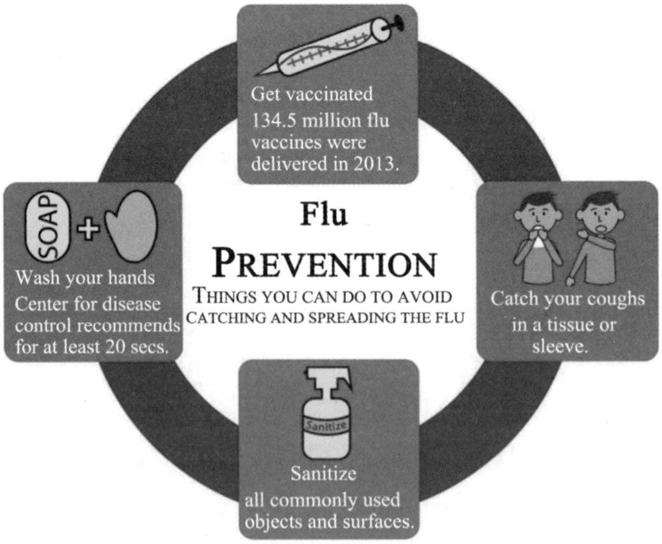

Pic. 1-3 Flu prevention

A5. Follow-up Activities

Group Talk

You are required to conduct a group talk on the topic: ***Do you know any one who can't eat something because of an allergy, and what will happen when the allergy attacks?*** After the talk, select one of you to share the most interesting story with the whole class.

You may refer to the expressions below, but don't confine yourself to them.

Suggested Expressions:

I have a bad allergy to animal hair.
My allergies are acting up.
I have seasonal allergies.
One's eyes are itchy.
One's sinuses are acting up.
What are the typical allergens?
Pollen (penicillin, nuts, sunshine, egg, etc.) makes one's allergies act up.
One can't stop sneezing.
One's nose is running. / One has a runny nose.
Blow one's nose.
Allergies run in one's family.

Story Sharing

Tell a story on the topic: ***Have you ever had a diarrhea that confines you at home?*** In your speaking, try to recall the past which truly happened to you, and describe the associated symptoms and causes of your sickness. You are suggested to use what you have learned in this unit to tell a full story.

Information Repeating

Read the information below and repeat it to the class with details.

The Interesting Diseases: Cyclic Vomiting Syndrome

"Cyclic vomiting syndrome (CVS)" sounds official and scientific, but look closely at that name; it means, basically, "throws up every so often." It just describes what's happening without any clue to the reason why. It's thought that CVS is linked somehow to migraines, as sufferers often have both and CVS sometimes respond to migraine medication, but mostly the official diagnosis consists of "Dunno... Magic?".

Having no obvious cause might be enough to get CVS on the list of interesting diseases all by itself, but what's really weird about it is its regularity. Vomiting episodes tend to happen, not necessarily in response to certain foods or medications (as with allergies), but instead at around the same time of day, as if the child was allergic to afternoons. Nobody knows why CVS strikes, how long it will last, or why it seems to clear up on its own over a period of months, years, or decades. We're going with magic.

(Adapted from *allthatsinteresting.com*)

Interpretation

Interpret the following paragraphs into English with what you have learned in Part A.

Paragraph 1

Wilson最近有些不舒服，于是去看医生。Wilson告诉医生，他最近总是头晕、恶心，还伴有失眠，也许是因为压力过大。医生为他测量了血压，发现他有严重的高血压。Wilson又去验血，结果显示他的血脂和血糖都很高。然后医生借助听诊器检查他的肺部，发现他呼吸不太平稳。最后，医生为他开了一些处方药，并嘱咐他规律作息、健康饮食、适当健身。如果病情加剧，应立即就医。

Paragraph 2

在日常生活中我们常面临意外的伤害，比如车祸或其他突发事故，这可能会导致出血、骨折等严重后果。此时，急救箱将发挥重要作用。对于关节脱臼或骨折，我们可使用纱布、绷带来固定和支撑伤处。在紧急情况下，伤者可能会晕厥，这时心肺复苏则是挽救生命的关键。另外，用于控制大出血的止血带也是急救箱里的必备物品。正确使用急救物品，可及时救治伤者，减少伤害并促进其快速康复。

Paragraph 3

我上周预约了今天去体检。在护士的引导下，我先完成了缴费，然后测量了身高和体重，结果显示我超重。接下来，医生对照视力表检查我的视力，发现视力再次下降，建议我不要长时间盯着屏幕。基础项目检查完之后，我又去采血室采血。正当我以为全部检查都结束时，护士告诉我还需去二楼做胸部X光检查。上楼时我突然感到一阵头晕，四肢无力。护士扶住了我，她说我脸色苍白，可能是贫血或低血糖，建议我等体检结果都出来后再去就诊。

A6. Extension

Synonym Discrimination

Can you figure out the differences among the words below?

Group 1: dizzy / lightheaded / dazzling / giddy
Group 2: hiccup / burp / belch
Group 3: shake / shiver / dither / tremble / shudder / quiver / quake

Group 4: pill / tablet / capsule / caplet / soft gel / granule / ointment / oral solution / fluid / effervescent tablet

Extensive Reading

Passage One

Recognizing Medical Emergencies

Getting medical help right away for someone who is having a medical emergency can save their lives. This article describes the warning signs of a medical emergency and how to be prepared.

Information

According to the American College of Emergency Physicians, the following are warning signs of a medical emergency:

- Bleeding that will not stop.
- Breathing problems (difficulty breathing, shortness of breath).
- Change in mental status (such as unusual behavior, confusion, difficulty arousing).
- Chest pain.
- Choking.
- Coughing up or vomiting blood.
- Fainting or loss of consciousness.
- Feeling of committing suicide or murder.
- Head or spine injury.
- Severe or persistent vomiting.
- Sudden injury due to a motor vehicle accident, burns or smoke inhalation, near drowning, deep or large wound, or other injuries.
- Sudden, severe pain anywhere in the body.
- Sudden dizziness, weakness, or change in vision.
- Swallowing a poisonous substance.
- Severe abdominal pain or pressure.

Be prepared:

- Determine the location and quickest route to the nearest emergency department before an emergency happens.
- Keep emergency phone numbers posted in your home where you can easily access them. Also enter the numbers into your cell phone. Everyone in your household, including children, should know when and how to call these numbers. These numbers include: fire department, police department, poison control center, ambulance center, your doctors' phone numbers, contact numbers of neighbors

or nearby friends or relatives, and work phone numbers.

- Know at which hospital(s) your doctor practices and, if practical, go there in an emergency.
- Wear a medical identification tag if you have a chronic condition, or look for one on a person who has any of the symptoms mentioned.
- Get a personal emergency response system if you're an older adult, especially if you live alone.

What to do if someone needs help:

- Stay calm, and call your local emergency number (such as 911).
- Start CPR (cardiopulmonary resuscitation) or rescue breathing, if necessary and if you know the proper technique.
- Place a semiconscious or unconscious person in the recovery position until the ambulance arrives. DO NOT move the person, however, if there has been or may have been a neck injury.
- Upon arriving at an emergency room, the person will be evaluated right away. Life- or limb-threatening conditions will be treated first. People with conditions that are not life- or limb-threatening may have to wait.

Call your local emergency number if:

- The person's condition is life-threatening (for example, the person is having a heart attack or severe allergic reaction).
- The person's condition could become life-threatening on the way to the hospital.
- Moving the person could cause further injury (for example, in case of a neck injury or motor vehicle accident).
- The person needs the skills or equipment of paramedics.
- Traffic conditions or distance might cause a delay in getting the person to the hospital.

(Adapted from *medlineplus.gov*)

Passage Two

Basic Emergency Response

All medical emergencies occurring on campus should be reported immediately by calling local police from a campus phone.

Medical emergencies include:

- Any life-threatening situation.
- Loss of consciousness.

- Chest pain.
- Excessive bleeding.
- Seizures.
- Head injury.
- Compound fractures.
- Allergic reactions with shortness of breath, excessive swelling.
- Ingestion or inhalation of a toxic substance.
- Lacerations of the eyeball.

Quick response:

- Dial university police.
- Do not move the victim unless safety dictates.
- If trained, use pressure to stop bleeding.
- Use CPR if no pulse and not breathing.

State that medical aid is needed and provide the following information:

- Location of injured person (e.g. which building, room, number, etc.).
- Type of injury or problem.
- The individual's present condition.
- The sequence of events leading to the emergency.
- Medical history and name of injured person's doctor, if known.
- The phone number and where you are.
- Stay on the phone with the dispatcher.

Personal Injury Procedures

Clothing on fire:

- Roll around on floor to smother flame or drench with water.
- Obtain medical attention; if necessary, call university police.
- Report incident to supervisor and / or the university police.

Hazardous material splashed in eye:

- Immediately rinse eyeball and inner surface of eyelid with water continuously for 15 minutes.
- Forcibly hold eye open to ensure wash behind eyelids.
- Obtain medical attention.
- Report incident to supervisor and / or the university police.

Minor cuts and puncture wounds:

- Vigorously wash injury with soap and water for several minutes.
- Obtain medical attention.

- Report incident to supervisor and / or the university police.

Radiation spill on body:

- Remove contaminated clothing.
- Rinse exposed area thoroughly with water.
- Obtain medical attention.
- Report incident to supervisor and / or the university police.

Biological spill on body:

- Remove contaminated clothing.
- Vigorously wash exposed area with soap and water for one minute.
- Obtain medical attention.
- Report incident to supervisor and / or the university police.

(Adapted from *emergency.appstate.edu*)

Part B Dental Health and Beauty

B1. Introduction

Why Dental Health Is Important ?

Practicing good dental health is important to maintaining a healthy mouth, teeth and gums. It will also help your appearance and quality of life.

Your dental health team consists of you and dental health professionals. Together, you can prevent many dental problems from causing a diminished quality of life and potential medical complications.

Your dental health professionals include:

- Dentist.
- Dental hygienist.

Dental specialists:

- Periodontist.
- Orthodontist.
- Oral and maxillofacial surgeons.

Diseased, crooked or missing teeth or a misshapen jaw can interfere with your speech; make chewing your food properly difficult and painful, and lead to expensive corrective procedures.

Cavities are painful places on your teeth where decay has eaten through the enamel and exposed a tooth's root. Hot or cold food or liquids can send a painful signal that something is wrong.

Cavities may not have any symptoms until after significant damage to the tooth. This is why regular visits to your dental professional are so important. Early signs of tooth decay are easier to treat than advanced cases.

Thanks to modern dental technology, treating tooth decay, especially in the early stages, is often only mildly uncomfortable, at its worse. Medications that numb the area of the decay eliminate the pain of filling a cavity for most people.

Complication

Another complication of poor oral health is gum disease, which can be mild in the initial stages, but lead to much more severe problems if untreated. Gum disease or periodontal disease may cause loss of teeth, infections and other complications.

In addition to complications for your teeth and gums, research has linked periodontal disease to other health problems including heart complications, strokes, diabetes complications and respiratory issues.

Good dental health is a combination of proper daily maintenance (brushing and flossing) along with regular visits to your dental care professional.

People with crooked teeth, misaligned jaws and other problems with their mouth can often benefit from orthodontic procedures, such as braces or other techniques to correct the problems.

Your dental health professional can help you decide how to address the problems. Braces, once for adolescents only, can help people of all ages correct problems with their teeth and jaws. Not only do orthodontic procedures help your appearance, but they can also improve chewing and proper digestion of food along with some speech problems.

Regular visits to your dental health professional help you maintain healthy teeth, gums and mouth.

(Adapted from *marshfieldclinic.org*)

B2. Words and Expressions

Vocabulary

1. deciduous /dɪˈsɪdʒuəs/ *adj*. (牙齿、鹿角等到达一定发育期后)脱落的,(树木)落叶的
2. canine /ˈkeɪnaɪn/ *adj*. 犬的,狗的
3. snaggletooth /ˈsnæɡltuːθ/ *n*. 暴牙,凸牙,断齿,参差不齐的牙齿

Types of Tooth	**牙齿类型**
baby tooth / milk tooth / deciduous tooth / primary tooth	乳齿,乳牙
permanent tooth	恒齿
front tooth	门牙,门齿
upper tooth	上牙,上齿
lower tooth	下牙,下齿
cheek tooth / molar	磨牙,臼齿

canine tooth	犬齿
tiger tooth	虎牙
wisdom tooth	智齿
bucktooth	獠牙,龅牙
snaggletooth	参差不齐的牙齿

Vocabulary

1. tartar /ˈtɑːrtə/ *n*. 牙石,牙垢
2. plaque /plæk/ *n*. 齿菌斑,牙斑
3. saliva /səˈlaɪvə/ *n*. 口水,唾液,涎
4. fluoride /ˈflɔːraɪd/ *n*. 氟化物
5. wax /wæks/ *n*. 蜡
6. rinse /rɪns/ *v*. (用清水)冲洗,涮洗,漂洗
7. gargle /ˈgɑːrgəl/ *v*. (尤指为了清洁口腔或止痛)漱口,漱喉,含漱

Dental Hygiene	**口腔卫生**
bad breath	口臭
gum	牙龈,牙床
saliva	口水,唾液,涎
electric toothbrush	电动牙刷
fluoride toothpaste	含氟牙膏
mouthwash	漱口水
teeth whitener	牙齿增白剂
whiten one's teeth	美白牙齿
toothpick	牙签
waxed floss	含蜡牙线
floss one's teeth	用牙线洁牙
slit between teeth	牙缝
rinse	冲洗,涮洗
gargle	漱口,含漱
dental hygienist	牙科医师,牙科保健医师
dental assistant	牙科助理,牙医助理
sensitive to hot and cold food	对冷热食物敏感
remove tartar buildup	去除牙石聚集
plaque	齿菌斑,牙斑
apply some fluoride	涂氟(防蛀)

Vocabulary

1. susceptible /səˈseptəbəl/ *adj*. 易受影响的，易受伤害的
2. canal /kəˈnæl/ *n*. 管，道
3. sew /soʊ/ *v*. 缝合(伤口)
4. anesthetic /ˌænəsˈθetɪk/ *n*. 麻醉剂
5. denture /ˈdentʃə/ *n*. 假牙，义齿(通常用作复数)

See a Dentist	**看牙医**
toothache	牙痛
tooth decay	蛀牙
gum pain / sore gum	牙龈疼痛
inflamed gum / infected gum	牙龈发炎
swollen gum	牙龈肿胀
susceptible to decay	易患蛀牙
mild infection	轻微感染
severe infection	重度感染
dental pulp may die	牙髓可能坏死
drill the cavity	钻洞
root canal treatment	根管治疗
fill a cavity	填牙洞
put in the filling	填牙，放入填充物
put a cap / crown on one's tooth	戴牙冠
have a tooth pulled / extracted / removed	拔牙
cotton ball	棉球
stitch	一针(缝纫的，编织的)
sew the gum	缝合牙龈
give one's gum an anesthetic injection	给牙龈注射麻药
give a shot of anesthetic	打一针麻醉剂
relieve / dull the pain	减轻疼痛
get an implant / implant a false tooth	植入假牙
wear a false tooth / wear dentures	戴假牙

Vocabulary

1. prenatal /ˌpriːˈneɪtəl/ *adj*. 产前的
2. heredity /həˈredəti/ *n*. 遗传
3. congenital /kənˈdʒenɪtl/ *adj*. 先天的，天生的，天赋的
4. embryologic /ˌembrɪəˈlɑːdʒɪk/ *adj*. 胚胎学的
5. thrust /θrʌst/ *v*. 推挤，刺，戳，插入

Causes of Dental Problems	**牙齿问题的起因**
prenatal development	孕期发育
heredity cause	遗传因素
race evolution	种族演化
congenital cause	先天因素
environmental cause	环境因素
disturbance in embryologic development	胚胎发育障碍
development disturbance	发育障碍
oral bacteria	口腔细菌
diet habit	饮食习惯
dental cleaning habit	牙齿清洁习惯
bad oral habit	不良口腔习惯
thumb sucking	吮指
tongue thrusting	吐舌，挺舌
lip habit	唇习惯

Vocabulary

1. orthodontist /ˌɔːrθoʊˈdɑːntɪst/ *n*. 牙齿矫正医师
2. palate /ˈpælət/ *n*. 上腭
3. variation /ˌverɪˈeɪʃən/ *n*. 变异，变种
4. aesthetic /esˈθetɪk/ *adj*. 美感的，审美的，美学的，美观的

See an Orthodontist	**看牙齿矫正医师**
irregular teeth	牙齿不规则
snaggle-toothed	牙齿参差不齐的
palate	上颚
jaw	下颚
variation	变异
medical history	病史
allergy history	过敏史
dental history	牙病史
treatment plan	正畸治疗计划
dental evaluation	牙齿检查
cleft (face, lip, jaw)	裂口,裂缝(脸、唇、鄂)
preventive orthodontics	预防矫治
interceptive orthodontics	阻断矫治
corrective orthodontics	一般矫治
surgical orthodontics	外科矫治
fixed appliance	固定矫治器
removable appliance	可摘矫治器
functional appliance	功能性矫治器
wear braces	戴牙套
aesthetic	美观的

B3. Situational Conversations

Conversation 1　Making an Appointment

P: Patient　D: Doctor's Office Assistant

D: Good morning, Beautiful Smile Dentistry, this is Jamie. How may I help you today?

P: Good morning, I'd like to **schedule a check-up.**

D: I'd be happy to do that for you. Have you been to Beautiful Smile before?

P: Yes, I have. My last check-up was six months ago.

D: Great. Can I get your name, please?

P: Yes, of course. My name is Joanne.

D: Thank you, Joanne. Which dentist did you see on your last check-up.

P: I'm not sure, really.

D: That's OK. Let me check your chart... Oh, Dr. Lee.

P: Yes, that's right.

D: OK... Dr. Lee will be available next Friday in the morning.

P: Hmm... that's not good. I've got work. How about the week after that?

D: Yes, Dr. Lee has some time open. Would you like to suggest a time?
P: Does he have any time open in the afternoon?
D: Yes, we could **fit you in** on Thursday, January 14th at 2:30 in the afternoon.
P: Great. That'll work.
D: OK, thank you for calling, we'll see you then.
P: Thank you, bye-bye.

(Adapted from *thoughtco.com*)

☞**Notes**

- **schedule a check-up**: If you don't feel well and want to see a dentist, you have to make an appointment in advance to do a check-up, and it is not just confined to dental check-up, but also for regular dental cleaning and any dental problems.
- **fit you in**: to find time to do or deal with something or someone.

Conversation 2 Doing a Dental Check-up

S: Sam D: Dentist
S: Hello, doctor.
D: Good morning, Sam. How are you doing today?
S: I'm OK. I've been having some gum pain recently.
D: Well, we'll take a look. Please **recline** and open your mouth... that's good.
S: (*after being examined...*) How does it look?
D: Well, there is some inflammation of the gums. I think we should also do a new set of X-rays.
S: Why do you say that? Is something wrong?
D: No, no, it's just **standard procedure** every year. It looks like you may have a few cavities as well.
S: That's not good news.
D: There are just two and they look superficial.
S: I hope so.
D: We need to take X-rays to identify other tooth decay and make sure that there isn't any between the teeth.
S: I see.
D: Here, put on this **protective apron**.
S: Okay.
D: (*after taking X-rays...*) Things look good. I don't see any evidence of further decay.
S: That's great!
D: Yes, I'll just get these two fillings **drilled** and taken care of and then we'll get your

teeth cleaned.

(Adapted from *thoughtco.com*)

☞ **Notes**

- **recline**: to lie or lean back with the upper part of your body in a nearly horizontal position.
- **standard procedure**: a set of written guidelines or instructions for the completion of a routine task, designed to increase performance, improve efficiency, and ensure quality through systemic homogenization.
- **protective apron**: something worn by a patient during an X-ray to keep them safe from the rays emitted by imaging equipment.
- **drill**: to use a special tool to remove bacteria from a cavity in order to prepare it for filling and prevent more decay.

Conversation 3 Keeping Dental Hygiene

S: Simon D: Dental Hygienist

S: Hello.

D: Hello, Mr. Simon Waters. I'm Gina. I'll be cleaning your teeth today.

S: Dr. Peterson has just filled two cavities. Why do I need a cleaning?

D: Well, we have to get your teeth and gums clean and **disease-free**.

S: I guess that makes sense.

D: Oral health leads to trouble-free teeth. I'll start off by removing plaque. Please lean back and open wide.

S: OK, I hope it's not too bad.

D: Everybody gets plaque, even if they floss regularly. That's why it's important to come in twice a year for check-ups.

S: (*getting his teeth cleaned, can't say much...*)

D: OK, please take a drink and rinse.

S: Ah, that's better.

D: OK, now I'll apply some **fluoride**. Which flavor would you like?

S: Do I have a choice?

D: Sure, we have mint, spearmint, orange or bubble-gum — that's for the kids.

S: I'd like to have the bubble-gum!

D: OK. (*applies fluoride*) Now, let me give your teeth a final flossing.

S: What type of **floss tape** do you recommend?

D: Personally, I like the flat tape. It's easier to get between the teeth.

S: OK, I'll remember that the next time I buy floss. How often should I floss?

D: Everyday! Twice a day if possible! Some people like to floss after every meal, but that's not absolutely necessary.

S: (*after finishing the cleaning...*) I feel much better. Thank you.

D: My pleasure. Have a pleasant day, and remember to floss every day — at least once a day!

(Adapted from *thoughtco.com*)

Notes

- **disease-free:** not suffering from, contaminated by or exposed to a particular disease.
- **fluoride:** a chemical substance, sometimes added to water or toothpaste, which is applied to help keep teeth healthy and avoid cavity. Mouth rinses containing fluoride in lower strengths are available over the counter; stronger concentrations require a doctor's prescription.
- **floss tape:** also named dental tape or ribbon tape, used for cleaning between the slits. Due to the broadness of floss tape, it is much easier as compared to dental floss. It is specially made for people who have braces.

B4. Picture Knowledge

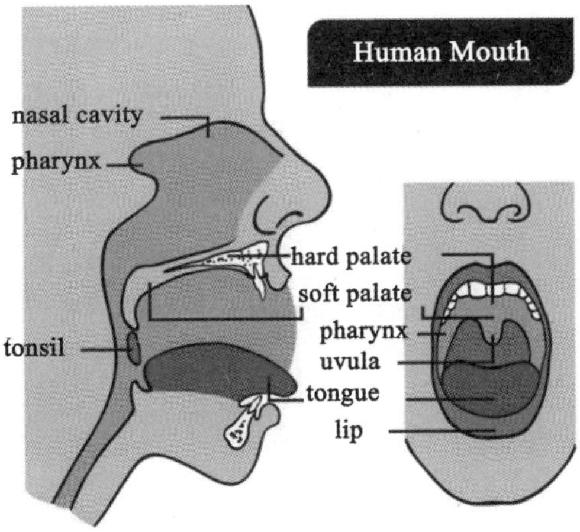

Pic. 1-4 Human mouth

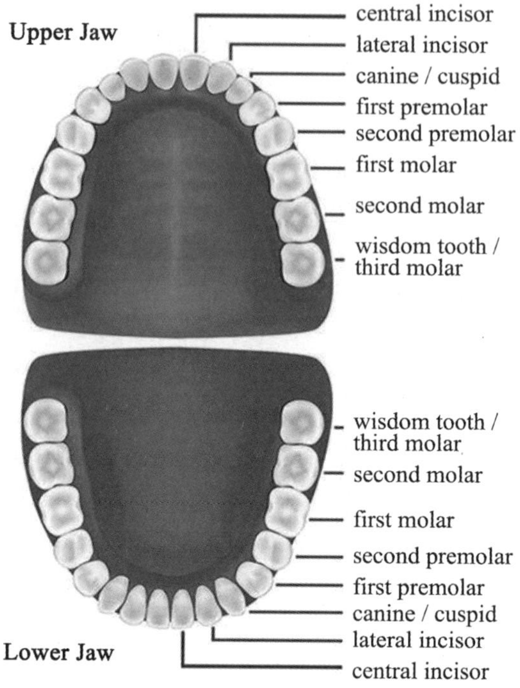

Pic. 1-5 Human teeth

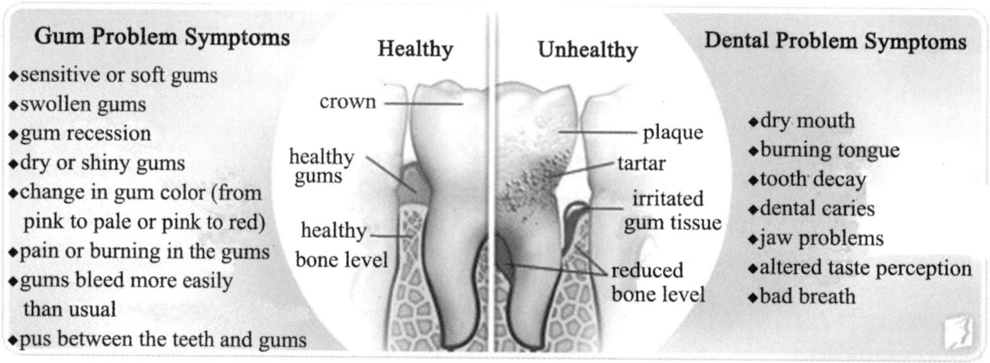

Pic. 1-6 Gum and dental problem symptoms

B5. Follow-up Activities

Story Sharing

Tell a story on the topic: ***The most unforgettable dental experience.*** In your speaking, try to recall the past which truly happened to you, and describe the associated symptoms and causes of your tooth problems. You are suggested to use what you have learned in this unit to tell a full story.

You may refer to the expressions below, but don't confine yourself to them.

Suggested Expressions:

One came in for a check-up and a dental cleaning.

Be here for a procedure.

One's tooth is sore.

One's tooth hurts.

One has a toothache.

One has this pain for about a week or so.

It bothers one when one eats something really cold.

It hurts a lot more when...

It hurts when it is touched.

One has got some bad decay in there.

There is a major cavity in there.

Fill that tooth.

Put a cap on one's tooth.

Extract the tooth.

Dull the pain.

Discussion

Imagine that you are an international student in the U.S., your irregular teeth make you rather unconfident. However, the expense of wearing braces is quite high in there. Taking into account those variations, insurance coverage and location, the average cost of braces for kids might be between $4,685 and $6,500, according to the American Dental Association (ADA). The typical expense of braces for grownups is $4,800 to $7,135. How would you make a decision in such a dilemma?

Conduct a group discussion on the topic: ***Will you spend a lot of money on wearing braces?*** Select one of you to stand for your group and summarize your viewpoints.

Interpretation

Interpret the following paragraphs into English with what you have learned in Part B.

Paragraph 1

最近我的朋友Rob去看牙医。经过X光拍照后医生发现,他的牙龈里长了一颗大智齿,而且是横向生长的,这会导致与智齿相邻的牙齿疼痛甚至排列不整齐。因此,医生建议拔掉这颗智齿以避免其他问题。

Paragraph 2

在拔牙前,医生需要先给Rob清洗牙齿,再进行牙龈麻醉。清洁过程中,医生发现Rob

不仅有智齿问题，而且智齿旁边还有颗蛀牙，需要在拔掉智齿后解决蛀牙问题。医生提出两个方案：第一，由于蛀牙腐坏严重，需借助锥子在牙齿上方开个小口，做好填充后，给牙齿戴上牙冠；第二，拔掉整颗蛀牙，再预约其他时间进行植牙。

Paragraph 3

两个方案各有利弊。第一个方案费用低、用时长，必须在没有麻醉的情况下进行根管治疗，这会引起较强的痛感。此外，牙冠的保质期在 5 年左右，后期容易松动脱落，还需再次更换。第二个方案副作用小，植牙保质期略长，但费用是第一个方案的 20 倍左右，还可能导致牙龈发炎。

Paragraph 4

除了每天早晚仔细刷牙以外，牙医还提醒 Rob 在日常牙齿养护中注意以下三点：第一，使用牙线以彻底清洁牙齿，早晚各一次；第二，使用漱口水以避免口臭，每次餐后漱口；第三，每年找牙医洗牙一次，通过清理牙结石和牙菌斑来保持口腔卫生。

Information Repeating

Read the information below and repeat it to the class in details.

American Obsession with Perfecting Their Teeth

Dan P. Lee

Over the past two decades, the number of North American teenagers in orthodontic treatment has nearly doubled, so that 80 percent are currently in an orthodontist's care, with the recommended average age of a first visit now 7. So it was perhaps inevitable that the population pool of potential customers would expand to include parents. Adults now make up roughly a quarter of all orthodontics patients in the U.S. and Canada.

Studies, mostly sponsored by dentists and orthodontists, regularly claim that life basically sucks for those with imperfect smiles. According to one survey from 2012, 38 percent of Americans would rule out a second date with someone with misaligned teeth, and those with straight teeth are 38 percent more likely to be perceived as smart. Americans supposedly prefer a nice smile to clear skin and are willing to go to great lengths to get one, even giving up dessert (39 percent) or vacations (37 percent).

(Adapted from *thecut.com*)

B6. Extension

Synonym Discrimination

Can you figure out the differences among the words below?

Group 1: rinse / gargle

Group 2: dental floss / toothpick
Group 3: cheek teeth / wisdom teeth

Extensive Reading

Passage One

Invisalign vs. Wire Braces

With 1 out of 5 Americans feeling anxiety and an unsettling impact on their mental wellbeing due to the condition of their teeth, the surge in the desire to receive corrective treatment is understandable. When considering options for teeth alignment, people often have queries related to the cost-effectiveness in terms of value provided by the various treatments available in the market.

However, what is more uncommonly known is that orthodontic treatments have a lasting impact on the overall periodontal health of the mouth post-procedure, which potential patients tend to overlook due to a lack of awareness. The level of discomfort one can expect from any orthodontic treatment, paired with the challenge of choosing the right dental solution can make the task extremely daunting.

With options like wire braces and the Invisalign treatment competing head to head, there are intrinsic mechanisms to each that must be ascertained over their blatant visual differences. A cross-sectional study on gingival parameters and patient satisfaction during treatment was conducted to highlight the potential pros and cons of braces and Invisalign treatments.

In a 6-month long scientific study conducted on 139 orthodontic patients aged between 11 to 62 years, subjects were screened for sulcus bleeding and plaque. All subjects were provided with the same oral hygiene conditions, while all patients underwent the same professional preventative hygiene treatment.

In clinical examinations, it was reported that Invisalign served as a better option to align teeth, with higher patient satisfaction scores, and lower gingival inflammation. In contrast, patients with braces suffered from increased plaque accumulation with a higher susceptibility to decalcifications and white spot lesions.

Invisalign or braces — which treatment is better for you

It is important to note the structural differences between both treatments prior to settling with one. Braces are considered as an invasive treatment, consisting of metal or porcelain brackets being glued to the teeth, with titanium or stainless steel wires pulling at them, creating a tightening and aligning effect.

Invisalign, on the other hand, comprises a sequence of clear liners; custom made to snugly fit each mouth. The ergonomics of these cause a movement in the teeth of about 1/4-millimeter, in the predetermined direction. With the aid of computer simulations, specialists decide the design and function of each aligner, bolstering the pattern of movement intended.

Costs

Patients with braces can expect to be set back anywhere between \$1800-6000 while complicated cases can cost up to \$10,000. Invisalign's clear liners are priced at \$3500-8000 and can be performed by an orthodontist, or a Dental GP with extensive experience.

This higher cost in comparison to braces is offset by the multiple benefits and conveniences it provides to the patient. Invisalign reduces the risk of periodontal decay and gingival inflammation, resulting in better oral conditions for the patients. This benefit extends from the removable design of the aligner tray.

Maintenance & cleaning

The brackets and wires used in traditional braces make the cleaning process difficult while its permanently glued nature requires additional cleaning equipment, such as special toothbrushes and water flossers to aid in the removal of debris and food particles that may stick to the wires. Invisalign's removable features allow more flexibility in keeping an effective and simple oral hygiene routine.

Poor cleaning habits can lead to decalcification, decay, cavities, and gum disorders in the future. Maintaining hygiene with Invisalign is fairly easy and straightforward; with you having to remove the aligners when eating or drinking anything other than water, before bed and when brushing or flossing to give you easier access to your teeth. Caring for your Invisalign aligners typically requires you to keep your trays clean and sanitized and change your aligners when scheduled.

Durability & reliability

While braces may seem sturdy, they can prove to be fragile when biting into something hard. The glue may give way if not applied with care or the wire could snap, requiring an emergency visit to the dentist.

Cases better suited for braces are forgetful individuals or younger children prone to misplacing things — given the removable nature of Invisalign. Braces are also suitable for patients requiring highly complex and technical teeth repositions or bite restructures. However, they have been known to cause slight discomfort, with cuts, bleeds, soreness, and even excruciating pain as reported by some patients.

Flexibility of use

Invisalign works in a way that provides flexibility of use, with no nicks and cuts. It is better suited for busy lifestyles, especially for teens and mature patients and even athletes. However, it does not cater to patients with severe back-tooth bite issues, bridgework, and other similar problems. Compliant patients who wear Invisalign for at least 20 continuous hours a day tend to see faster results; however, the forçe of both braces and Invisalign determines the speed of the treatment's progress.

The verdict

Invisalign reduces the possibility of oral health related issues which may occur with a mismanaged hygiene routine owing to the inflexible nature of braces. While both dental treatments are considered excellent for treating misaligned teeth, for people looking for a more comfortable solution with an easier oral hygiene regimen and maximum benefits — Invisalign proves to be the better choice.

The chances of tooth decay with traditional procedures are higher, making the cost saved on acquiring the procedure ineffective in the long run; the resulting orthodontic conditions may require even costlier treatments to counteract the damage.

Paying attention to your dental habits and arranging regular appointments with a trusted dentist can extend the life of your teeth.

(Adapted from *orchardscottsdental.com*)

Passage Two

Dental Costs with and without Insurance

Everyone needs dental care at some point. However, not everyone wants to pay for insurance coverage. Chances are you've thought about costs tied to proper treatment. If you're considering covering dental costs out-of-pocket on a pre-treatment basis, knowing common procedure costs is important. While avoiding upfront costs from purchasing a dental insurance plan may seem cost-effective, having a great dental plan can greatly reduce your overall cost of care.

Check-ups

Common check-up and cleaning costs vary. Dentists charge different rates depending on your situation and where you live. In most places, an average check-up costs about $288, which covers an exam, X-rays, and cleaning.

Fillings

Fillings, while more expensive than basic dental check-ups, both fix cavities and protect your mouth's future health. Most filling treatments hold stable prices in the following ranges:

- $ 50 to $ 150 for a single, silver amalgam filling.
- $ 90 to $ 250 for a single, tooth-colored composite filling.
- $ 250 to $ 4,500 for a single, cast-gold or porcelain filling.

In most cases, prices may increase if a filling is "hard to reach". A back molar, an impacted tooth or other complications may cost more than a simple filling for a front tooth.

Tooth extractions

"Non-surgical" extractions and "surgical" extractions are needed when a tooth can't be repaired. Treatment costs depend on the visit's length and difficulty. In general, both non-surgical and surgical extractions need anesthesia. Average tooth removals cost:

- $ 75 to $ 300 for non-surgical, gum-erupted tooth extraction.
- $ 150 to $ 650 for a surgical extraction utilizing anesthesia.
- $ 185 to $ 600 for soft tissue and complicated surgical extractions.
- $ 75 to $ 200 for wisdom tooth extraction.

Impacted teeth can also boost costs up to $ 600, depending upon the tooth's location.

Crowns

While fillings are needed to block off a tooth's internal damages, crowns protect a tooth's "outside area". Crown placement normally follows a root canal treatment, and a crown's cost is tied to the base's material. Crowns can vary widely on materials used and, subsequently, cost:

- an average $ 328 per single resin crown.
- an average $ 821 per single porcelain-fused crown.
- an average $ 776 per single full cast high noble metal crown.

Root canals

Root canal treatment and impacted tooth "root cutting" are used on patients with exposed, infected or damaged tooth roots. Most often, root canal treatment costs are tied to the procedure's difficulty.

- an average $ 120 for a single, exposed root removal procedure.
- an average $ 185 for a single, residual tooth root removal procedure.

Does dental insurance save money

Dental services can be expensive. Many patients try to avoid dental expenditures by avoiding dental insurance altogether. While dental insurance coverage does typically require a monthly or annual premium, and some upfront costs or co-payments, in most cases, dental insurance actually lowers a person's overall dental costs. Patients with "average" dental plans can reduce their costs by the following amounts:

- 100 percent of costs for annual routine care.
- 80 percent of costs for fillings, basic procedures, and root canals.
- 50 percent of costs for bridges, crowns, and other major procedures.

There are more dental insurance options than ever before, so finding the right plan to balance your costs vs. savings is possible. The world of great dental care is here, and dental insurance can protect your teeth and bank account. Avoid high-cost dental procedures and browse the marketplace today to locate the dental insurance coverage that's right for you.

(Adapted from *memberbenefits.com*)

Sources of Pictures

Pic. 1-1 Retrieved from *en.islcollective.com*
Pic. 1-2 Retrieved from *englishstudyhere.com*
Pic. 1-3 Retrieved from *byuicomm.org*
Pic. 1-4 Retrieved from *findrighthealth.com*
Pic. 1-5 Retrieved from *vcdental.com.au*
Pic. 1-6 Retrieved from *westbowmanvilledental.com*

References

M. D. Lissa Rankin. (2020). Physical Signs That You Shouldn't Ignore. *Mindbodygreen*. Retrieved from https://www.mindbodygreen.com/0—9853/12-signs-youre-unhealthy-that-you-probably-ignore-but-shouldnt.html.

Anil. Talking about Stomachache. *Lemongrad*. Retrieved from https://lemongrad.com/conversation-between-doctor-and-patient/on July 12th, 2021.

Kenneth Beare. (2020). A Physical Examination. *ThoughtCo*. Retrieved from https://www.thoughtco.com/english-for-medical-a-physical-examination-1211327.

Richard Stockton. (2015). The Interesting Diseases: Cyclic Vomiting Syndrome. *Allthatsinteresting*. Retrieved from http://allthatsinteresting.com/interesting-diseases/2.

Recognizing Medical Emergencies. *National Library of Medicine*. Retrieved from https://medlineplus.gov/ency/article/001927.htm on July 12th, 2021.

Basic Emergency Responses. *Appalachian State University*. Retrieved from https://emergency.appstate.edu/basic-emergency-responses on July 12th, 2021.

Why Dental Health Is Important. *Marshfield Clinic Health System*. Retrieved from https://www.marshfieldclinic.org/specialties/dental-care/dental-why-importanton July 12th, 2021.

Kenneth Beare. (2019). Making an Appointment. *ThoughtCo*. Retrieved from https://www.thoughtco.com/making-an-appointment-with-the-dentist-1210349.

Kenneth Beare. (2019). Doing a Dental Checkup. *ThoughtCo*. Retrieved from https://www.thoughtco.com/dental-check-up-1210348.

Kenneth Beare. (2019). Keeping Dental Hygiene. *ThoughtCo*. Retrieved from https://www.thoughtco.com/dental-hygiene-dialogue-1210350.

Dan P. Lee. (2015). American Obsession with Perfecting Their Teeth. *The Cut*. Retrieved from https://www. thecut. com/2015/06/why-is-america-obsessed-perfect-teeth.html.

Invisalign vs. Wire Braces. *Orchard Scotts Dental*. Retrieved from https://www.orchardscottsdental.com/invisalign-vs-wire-braces/on July 12th, 2021.

Dental Costs with and without Insurance. *MemberBenefits*. Retrieved from https://memberbenefits.com/dental-costs-with-and-without-insurance/on July 12th, 2021.

Unit 2 Epidemic

Part A Causes and Symptoms

A1. Introduction

Introduction to Global Epidemics

Usually, there are four main types of diseases: infectious diseases, deficiency diseases, hereditary diseases, and physiological diseases. In terms of the transmission chance of any disease, it can either be communicable or noncommunicable. Communicable diseases are mostly infectious diseases, which introduced the epidemic phenomenon into the world a long time ago. A very rare disease that does not occur randomly in a population is usually categorized as an epidemic. The term epidemic originates from two Greek words: "epi-" meaning "upon", and "demos-" meaning "population". According to World Health Organization (WHO), a regional outbreak of an illness that spreads unexpectedly is known as an epidemic. The broad definition of epidemic disease delivered by the Centers for Disease Control and Prevention is "the occurrence of large number cases of disease, injury, or other health condition than expected in a given community or region or among a specific group of persons during a particular period."

There are three major components of an epidemiologic triad: external agent, susceptible host, and environment. The agent means an infectious pathogen such as a virus, bacterium, parasite, or other microbes that can attack the host in a favorable and balanced environment. All these three components work together to cause disease and other health events. The assessment of the interactions among these three components is required for developing effective interventions to control an epidemic.

There are four phases of an epidemic: the emergence of a disease in a community, outbreak of the disease with localized transmission, sustained outbreak of the disease in the community, and reduced transmission by controlling the disease or acquiring immunity. The epidemic concept is different from the other related infectious disease terms like "endemic", "outbreak", and "pandemic" in terms of the spreading of the disease. An endemic disease belongs to a particular geographic area. For example, malaria was an endemic disease in parts of Africa. An outbreak deals with an increase in the number of endemic cases and becomes an epidemic if not controlled quickly. The terms "epidemic" and "outbreak" are sometimes used interchangeably. While a disease-causing agent is different from current strains and much more infectious, the epidemic disease spreads over multiple countries by affecting a substantial number of people, and thus a situation, named a pandemic, arises. In general, pandemics affect far more people than an epidemic in wider geographical areas in the entire world and cause impaired health and many more deaths than epidemics, which often creates enormous social disruption, economic loss, and hardship.

The 21st century has been vigorously attacked by so many major epidemics, such as the SARS outbreak. The sign of SARS infection is similar to that of atypical pneumonia, and its symptoms are mainly breathing difficulties along with dry cough, fever, and headache. The case fatality rate (CFR) of the SARS epidemic was 11%. A decade later, the most severe Ebola epidemic since 1976 that caused a large number of deaths occurred in West Africa from December 2013 to January 2016. The average CFR of Ebola virus disease is about 50%, which indicates that the disease has a high risk of death. The incubation period of this disease is from 2 days to 3 weeks, while its major signs and symptoms are fever, sore throat, muscular pain, headaches, vomiting, diarrhea, decreased liver and kidney functions, sometimes internal and external bleeding, and low blood pressure from fluid loss. Now, with the COVID-19 still alive, a novel epidemic has emerged, the monkeypox. Caused by the monkeypox virus, it can result in a painful rash, enlarged lymph nodes, and fever. Most people fully recover, but some get very sick. For example, their skin can become infected with bacteria leading skin damage. Other complications include pneumonia, corneal infection with loss of vision, pain or difficulty swallowing, vomiting causing severe dehydration or malnutrition, sepsis, inflammation of the brain, or death.

As the current world remains vulnerable to epidemic events, the possibility of the next global pandemic could not be ignored. And since diseases very rarely disappear, there is always space for new ones. There are some reasons behind emerging and reemerging new pathogens and the increasing transmissibility and severity of infectious diseases. The major potential factors that serve as the breeding grounds for concerns of the future transmission of respiratory and fecal-oral pathogens are overpopulation; weak populations along with malnutrition in low-to-middle-income countries; quick and extreme mobility of individuals; greater interconnectivity between megacities; poverty; globalization; relentless urbanization; swelling populations of city dwellers; global warming; environmental degradation; ecological changes; habitat destruction; close and rehashed interaction among individuals, animals, and livestock; drug resistance to entering pathogens and the existence of viral pathogens with quick adaptation capacity to human hosts. Given the above-mentioned contributing factors, it is almost certain that the following arising infection will likewise spread quickly and far.

(Adapted from *ncbi.nlm.nih.gov*)

A2. Words and Expressions

Vocabulary

1. endemic /en'demɪk/ *n.* & *adj.* 地方性的;地方病
2. epidemic /epɪ'demɪk/ *n.* & *adj.* 传染病(的),流行病(的)
3. pandemic /pæn'demɪk/ *n.* & *adj.* 流行病(全国或全球性),瘟疫
4. pathogen /'pæθədʒən/ *n.* 病原体
5. strain /streɪn/ *n.* 毒株
6. interaction /ɪntə'rækʃə/ *n.* 相互作用
7. precipitation /priːˌsɪpə'teɪʃən/ *n.* (尤指雨或雪的)降落;降水
8. fragile /'frædʒəl/ *adj.* 易损坏的;易碎的;脆弱的
9. sewage /'suːɪdʒ/ *n.* 污水;污物
10. malnutrition /mælnuː'trɪʃən/ *n.* 营养不良

Source and Contributing Factors	**起源和影响因素**
endemic	地方性的;地方病
epidemic	传染病(的),流行病(的)
pandemic	流行病(全国或全球性),瘟疫
bacteria	细菌
fungi	真菌
microorganism	微生物
mould	霉菌
prion	朊病毒
variant	变体;变种
antigenic change	抗原变化
drug resistance	耐药性

pathogen	病原体
strain	毒株
proliferate	迅速繁殖
illegal wildlife trade	非法野生动物交易
fragile ecosystems	脆弱的生态系统
climate change	气候变化
global warming	全球气候变暖
break down the balance	打破平衡
melting of ice caps	冰冠融化
changing humidity	湿度变化
deforestation	森林砍伐
air and water pollution	空气和水污染
changing vegetation	植被变化
drought	干旱
flooding	洪水
irregular precipitation	不规则的降水
cross-species interaction	物种间的交互
shrinking habitats	栖息地缩小
local niche environment	当地适宜环境
distribution of vector organisms	病媒生物的分布
urbanization	城市化
agricultural expansion	农业扩张
land usage	土地使用
population growth and density	人口增长和密度
widespread travel	广泛旅行
sewage disposal	污水处理
immigration	移民
displace	转移；流离失所
host refugees	接收难民
overcrowded shelters	过度拥挤的避难所
poorly-equipped health institutions	设备简陋的医疗机构
post-disaster living conditions	灾后生活条件
malnutrition	营养不良
food-insecure	食品保障不足的
absence of supervision	监管缺失
delayed response	响应不及时

Vocabulary

1. outbreak /ˈaʊtbreɪk/ *n.* 爆发(战争);发作(疾病)
2. emergency /ɪˈmɜːdʒənsi/ *n.* 紧急情况;突发事件;非常时刻
3. incubation /ɪŋkjuˈbeɪʃn/ *n.* 孵化;[病毒][医]潜伏
4. transmissibility /trænzmɪsəˈbɪləti/ *n.* 可传染性;遗传性
5. inhalation /ˌɪnhəˈleɪʃən/ *n.* 吸气;吸入
6. transfusion /trænsˈfjuːʒən/ *n.* 输血;输液
7. mortality /mɔːrˈtæləti/ *n.* 死亡数量,死亡率;必死性
8. splash /splæʃ/ *v.* (使)(液体)洒,溅,泼
9. secretion /sɪˈkriːʃən/ *n.* 分泌;分泌液
10. stagnant /ˈstægnənt/ *adj.* (水或空气)不流动的,污浊的

Transmission	**传播**
outbreak	爆发(战争);发作(疾病)
emergency	紧急情况;突发事件;非常时刻
prevalence	(疾病等的)流行程度;普遍
transmissibility	可传染性;遗传性
route of transmission	传播途径
aerosol transmission	气溶胶传播
airborne	空气传播的
droplet transmission	飞沫传播
contact transmission	接触传播
zoonosis	人畜共患病
faecal-oral transmission	粪口传播
close contact	亲密接触(者)
community transmission	社区传播
mother-to-child transmission	母婴传播
delivery	分娩
breast feeding	母乳喂养
transfusion	输血;输液
blood and body fluids	血液和体液
formite	污染物

contaminate	污染
infectious	传染的，有传染性的
infectious agent	传染因子
infectious period	传染期
ingestion	摄取
inhalation	吸入
respiratory droplets	呼吸道飞沫
respiratory secretions	呼吸道分泌物
vector	带菌者
incubation period	潜伏期
at-risk population	高危人群
super-spreader	超级传播者
incubation period	潜伏期
virus carrier	病毒携带者
reagent	试剂，反应物
screen out	筛选出
positive	阳性的；确定的
negative	阴性的；否定的
mortality	死亡率
survival rate	存活率
high-occurrence season	高发季节
cross-contamination	交叉感染
communal facilities	公共设施
surfaces that are frequently-touched	经常接触的表面
share personal items	共用个人物品
frequent contact with dust and dirt	经常接触灰尘和污垢
mowing the lawn	修剪草坪
handle waste or anything else icky	处理垃圾或其他恶心的东西
garbage	湿垃圾
trash	干垃圾
touch animals or pets	触摸动物或宠物
animal feces	动物粪便
animal bites or scratches	动物咬伤或抓伤
poor personal hygiene	不良个人卫生
pick one's nose	挖鼻孔
rub one's eyes	揉眼睛

bite one's nails	咬指甲
go barefoot in the hospital	在医院内赤脚
nose blowing	擤鼻涕
split everywhere	随地吐痰
undercooked / underdone meat	未煮熟的肉
contaminated food or water	受污染的食物或水
decayed food	腐烂的食物
food debris	食物残渣
used needles	用过的针头
unprotected cuts	没有包扎的伤口
wound secretions	伤口分泌物
invasive medical devices	侵入性医疗器械
stagnant water	死水；积水
turbid water	浑水
cesspool	污水坑，污水池
water splash	水花飞溅
skin exposure	皮肤暴露
swim in a dirty river	在污水河里游泳
public bath	公共浴池

Vocabulary

1. myalgia /maɪˈældʒə/ *n*. [医]肌痛
2. sequela /sɪˈkwiːlə/ *n*. 后遗症
3. abscess /ˈæbses/ *n*. 脓肿
4. imperative /ɪmˈperətɪv/ *adj*. 极重要的；紧急的；迫切的
5. physiological /ˌfɪzɪəˈlɑːdʒɪkəl/ *adj*. 生理学的
6. exacerbate /ɪɡˈzæsəbeɪt/ *v*. 使恶化；使加重
7. detrimental /ˌdetrəˈmentəl/ *adj*. 有危害的，有损害的
8. ravage /ˈrævɪdʒ/ *n*. & *v*. 毁坏；蹂躏；掠夺
9. pessimistic /ˌpesəˈmɪstɪk/ *adj*. 悲观的
10. collapse /kəˈlæps/ *v*. 崩溃，垮掉

Symptoms	症状
immune system	免疫系统
severe	严重的
acute	急性的
syndrome	综合征
complication	并发症
mild symptoms	轻症
severe or critical condition	重症
asymptomatic	无症状的
physiological function	生理功能
loss of taste and smell	失去味觉和嗅觉
have no appetite	丧失食欲
organ failure	器官衰竭
lung lesion	肺部病变
breath with difficulty	呼吸困难
upper respiratory infection	上呼吸道感染
abscess	脓肿
fester	(伤口)化脓,溃烂
swelling of the lymph nodes	淋巴结肿大
myalgia	肌肉疼痛
chest tightness	胸闷
hemoptysis	咯血
edema	水肿
sequela	后遗症
amnesia	健忘(症)
unresponsive	反应迟缓的
sleep disorders	睡眠障碍
impaired taste and smell	嗅觉味觉异常

Impacts	影响
contingency plan	应急预案
powerless	无能为力的
exacerbate	使恶化;使加重
vulnerable groups	弱势群体

imperative	极重要的；紧急的
calamity	灾难；灾祸
dread	害怕；担心
salient threat	显著的威胁
persistent	持续的；顽强存在的
lifestyle changes	生活方式的变化
obsessive-compulsive disorder (OCD)	强迫症
psychological burden	心理负担
emotionally volatile	情绪不稳定的
languid	无精打采的
grief	悲痛，悲伤
anxiety	焦虑
pessimistic	悲观的
social exclusion	社会排斥
developmental downtime	发展停滞期
socioeconomic instability	社会经济不稳定
widespread job losses	大范围失业
business closures	企业倒闭
economic recession	经济衰退
function	运转；起作用
deceased	死亡的，去世的；逝者
detrimental	有危害的，有损害的
inflict	使遭受，使承受
function	运转；起作用
severe and durable	严重持久的
deteriorate	恶化，变坏
adverse	不利的；有害的
collapse	崩溃
susceptible	易受影响的，易受伤害的
deficient	缺乏的，缺少的
demographic	人口统计学的；人口的
ravage	毁坏；蹂躏；掠夺
lethal	致命的
lack of peer-to-peer communication	缺少与同伴的交流

disrupted daily rhythm 作息紊乱
stress reaction 应急反应
reflect on the past 反思过去
learn from the experience 汲取经验
get back on track 重回正轨；重振旗鼓

A3. Situational Conversations

Conversation 1 Talking about Zoonotic Diseases

C: Cynthia D: Dr. Findlay

C: Dr. Findlay, let's start by giving our listeners a brief explanation of zoonotic diseases.

D: Yes, of course. Zoonotic diseases are germs from viruses and bacteria that are passed from animals to humans. These viruses can spread quite quickly. This means they can easily jump from one region to another. In the past 20 years we have had several serious viruses around the world such as SARS, MERS, H1N1, Bird flu, and **West Nile virus.**

C: How do these viruses pass from animals to humans?

D: The first is direct contact, perhaps being bitten or scratched by an animal. It could also be coming in contact with an animal's urine or blood. It could also be caused by touching places that have germs from the animals, such as a barn or soil. Another way is eating food that is not safe, for example, eating raw or underdone meat or eggs.

C: Have most of these viruses come from the same animals?

D: No. They are different. For example, Middle Eastern respiratory syndrome (MERS) comes from camels. The H1N1 virus first appeared on a pig farm in Mexico. Bird flu was first found in geese and ducks on a farm in China. Viruses are also carried by mosquitoes in certain regions. For example, the West Nile virus is caused by a mosquito bite.

C: So what has made these viruses come to humans?

D: There are a few things that researchers believe may have caused these viruses to jump from animals to humans. One is fast growth in population. Other causes are environmental destruction and **industrial agriculture.** When environment is destroyed and developed, humans come into closer contact with animals. This also happens with farming, especially large farms. In the past 50 years, agriculture has become much **intensive** and animals are being raised very close to each other. This makes it easier for viruses to spread from animals to humans.

C: Is anything being done to try and control this?

D: Yes, people in the field of studying viruses are in close contact with each other. So if a virus suddenly appears in one part of the world, it is monitored and information passed to regional health offices as well as the World Health Organization.

C: That is good to know that science is trying to **keep on top of** this. Well, I would like to thank you for your time today.

D: Thank you for having me.

(Adapted from *linguahouse.com*)

☞**Notes**

- **West Nile virus**: a single-stranded RNA virus that causes West Nile fever, and this virus is primarily transmitted by mosquitoes.
- **industrial agriculture**: a form of modern farming that refers to the industrialized production of crops and animals and animal products like eggs or milk. The methods of industrial agriculture include innovation in agricultural machinery and farming methods, genetic technology, techniques for achieving economies of scale in production, the creation of new markets for consumption, the application of patent protection to genetic information, and global trade.
- **keep on top of (sb. / sth.)**: to be continuously aware of it and give it your regular attention.
- **intensive**: involving the maximum use of land, time, or some other resource.

Conversation 2 Talking about Two Different Endings of Epidemic

S: **Sam** **N**: **Neil**

S: In March 2020, the WHO, declared COVID-19 a pandemic. Now, after more than three years in the shadow of COVID-19, for many people travel restrictions are ending, and many people around the world are starting their lives again.

N: Yes, everyone now wants to see an end to the pandemic, whether it's because of lockdown and not seeing friends, or getting sick, even dying. But with cases of COVID infections still in the millions and doctors warning about new variants of the disease, is the pandemic really coming to an end?

S: In ancient times, it is hard to say pandemic can be totally ended or come to an end.

For example, in the Middle Ages, **the Black Death** that killed over half of Europe's population lasted for four years. It's only with modern vaccines that this disease has been **eradicated.**

N: You know there is a new idea that, it's not just the biological disease that needs to end, pandemics have a social ending too.

S: **Intriguing**, can you explain more about it?

N: Of course. Pandemics are not just a biological phenomenon, they're also a social phenomenon, and they end socially. And one of the ways that they end socially is when everyone just agrees that they have ended and is simply willing to tolerate more risks. In other words, we declare victory, maybe prematurely, or another way of thinking about it is, we **bury our heads in the sand.**

S: So, biologically, COVID still exists in the world and most of us would rather not catch it. But if we're vaccinated, the risk of getting seriously ill is much lower. In this sense, it's reasonable for us to make plans to **resume** normal life. And when enough people do this, we declare victory, which actually means that the pandemic finally has a social ending.

N: That's right. However, the danger is that we declare victory too **prematurely**, before it's the best time to do so.

S: And more important, pandemics do not end in the same way for everyone, everywhere. We are all clear that rich western countries with the resources to vaccinate their populations are in a better position than less developed countries.

N: Yes, and I intent to compare COVID pandemic to an ongoing disease which has killed millions, **rabies.**

S: I agree with your point. I have learned that what happens in the case of rabies is that it became from being an immediate **death sentence** basically to a preventable disease, but that happens in societies that have the means and the infrastructure to make that possible with vaccination, and that is not necessarily true for all parts of the world. Nevertheless, we don't think about the rabies as an ongoing epidemic.

N: Exactly, although rabies has extremely high mortality, modern vaccination allow people to prevent it effectively. And we now view rabies as a disease which can be prevented and controlled, rather than a death sentence.

S: To summarize, finding the right balance of COVID restrictions for communities of people **exhausted** by the pandemic isn't easy. Many scientists are warning that we haven't yet reached the beginning of the end of COVID, but hopefully we're at least reaching the end of the beginning.

(Adapted from *BBC.co.uk*)

☞ **Notes**

- **the Black Death**: a bubonic plague pandemic occurring in Western Eurasia and North Africa from 1346 to 1353, and it is the most fatal pandemic recorded in human history.
- **to bury one's heads in the sand**: to avoid, or try to avoid, a particular situation by pretending that it does not exist.
- **death sentence**: a legal judgment that a person shall be put to death following a criminal conviction literally; and by extension, that which ensures the death, destruction, ruin, or failure of someone or something.
- **eradicate**: to get rid of something completely or destroy something bad.
- **intriguing**: arousing great interest or curiosity.
- **resume**: to begin again or go on with something adjourned or interrupted.
- **prematurely**: in a way that happens or is done too soon, especially before the natural or suitable time.
- **exhaust**: to drain the energy of someone, or tire someone out.
- **rabies**(狂犬病): a preventable viral disease most often transmitted through the bite of a rabid animal. The rabies virus infects the central nervous system of mammals, ultimately causing disease in the brain and death.

Conversation 3 An Interview with Virologist John H. Connor

I: Interviewer C: John H. Connor

I: What kind of virus is monkeypox?

C: An orthopoxvirus (正痘病毒). It carries its genome as double-stranded DNA. It is similar to other known human pathogens like cowpox.

I: What do we know and not know about the modes of monkeypox transmission and the groups that are most impacted at this time?

C: Past studies have suggested that monkeypox virus can be transmitted from person to person by direct contact with monkeypox rash lesions, scabs, or body fluids, and respiratory droplets. In addition, contact with infected rodents can lead to infection. There are studies showing the presence of monkeypox DNA on surfaces, and that under the right conditions, it can be present for hours to days. However, as yet, there is no evidence that contaminated surfaces are responsible for transmission in the current outbreak in non-endemic areas. We do not know whether asymptomatic transmission can occur, although there is one study published as a **preprint** that suggests that this might be possible. **Wastewater testing** is being evaluated as a strategy for monkeypox surveillance. This looks **promising.**

I: OK, so knowing what we know about monkeypox, and knowing that not everybody today is vaccinated against monkeypox, how concerned should we be as we read about this new virus in our midst?

C: From my standpoint, people should be aware. But I am not **heading for the hills.** The basis for that is while monkeypox can be transmitted person to person, it is not something that has been described as having the really **wildfire** transmission we have seen with COVID-19. There has been an ongoing outbreak of monkeypox in Nigeria since 2017, and there are only 500 or 600 cases.

I: The average length of isolation for people who contract monkeypox is two to four weeks, are you worried that this extensive isolation period may significantly disrupt daily life if cases continue to rise?

C: The recovery time and isolation period is long. Aside from the pain associated with monkeypox itself, the extended isolation is likely to place an additional mental and financial burden on individuals. The response to the current outbreak should include support for individuals during this period to address or **mitigate** these additional burdens.

I: Emerging infectious diseases have been on the rise for decades, but it seems as if we are seeing a particular **spike** in new or previously contained diseases, from COVID-19 and monkeypox to the new **Langya virus.** Is this activity unusual or a sign of improvement in disease surveillance?

C: The world is changing and many different factors, including climate change, environmental damage, changes in land use, consumption of exotic foods, urbanization, population growth, ease of global travel, war, and **displacement of populations**, all influence the risk of emergence of novel pathogens. We also have strengthened surveillance systems in many parts of the world such that we are better able to identify outbreaks of novel pathogens or a resurgence in old problems like polio, although we need to continue to strengthen infectious disease surveillance systems in many low- and middle-income countries.

(Adapted from *bu.edu*)

☞**Notes**

- **wastewater testing**: a method to quickly assess pathogens and chemical exposures among thousands of people in the community by sampling and testing wastewater, the combination of household sewage, industrial runoff, and sometimes storm water.
- **head for the hills**: to flee hastily, or to move to higher ground, as in preparation for or response to a natural disaster.
- **Langya virus**: a species of henipavirus first detected in the Chinese provinces of Shandong and Henan. It has been announced in 35 patients from 2018 to August 2022, with the symptoms including fever, fatigue, and cough.
- **displacement of populations**: the relocation of large numbers of people from their homes, which is not only caused by environmental changes, but often occurs because of inequitable social and political systems that do not provide people with protection, food, clean water, and healthcare.
- **preprint**: a piece of academic work that is published but has not yet been assessed by other experts.
- **promising**: to be successful or enjoyable.
- **wildfire**: equals to very rapid and uncontrollable in some situations.
- **mitigate**: to make something less harmful, unpleasant, or bad.
- **spike**: a very high amount, price, or level, usually before a fall.

A4. Picture Knowledge

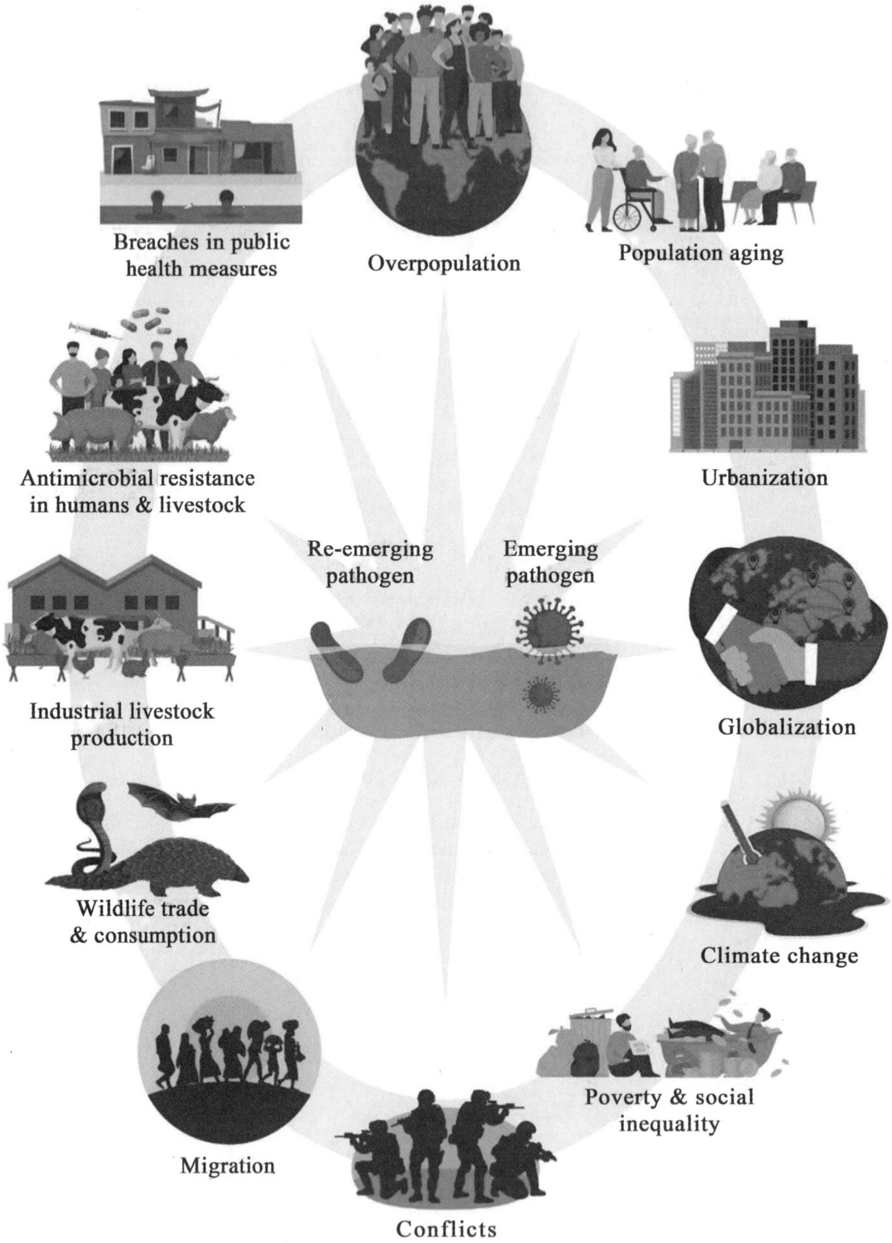

Pic. 2-1 Factors that contributing to the occurrence and transmission of emerging epidemics and re-emerging epidemics

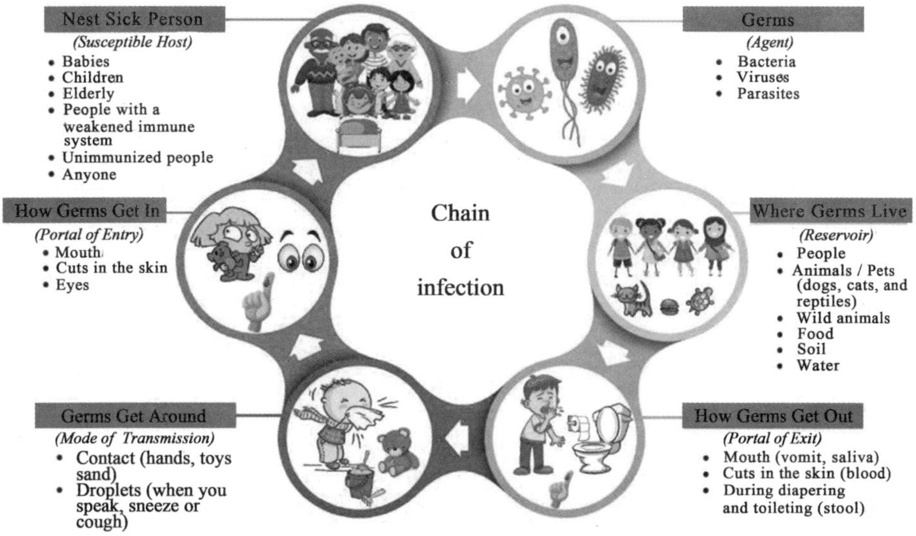

Pic. 2-2 Chain of infection

A5. Follow-up Activities

Partner Talk

As we grow up, we must have suffered from some common infectious diseases such as flu, mumps, measles, etc. Which disease affected you the most? How did you feel about it and overcome it? You are required to conduct a talk with your partners, and share your experience with the whole class.

Group Discussion

Along with the swift social development, we have seen more frequent epidemic outbreaks than before. From your own perspective, is there any relationship between human activities and epidemics? Conduct a group discussion and summarize your viewpoints.

Story Sharing

Share your story on the topic: The outbreak of COVID-19 has exerted a great impact on the lives and health of people all over the world. When it comes to our personal life in the past three years, what symptoms did you experience after contracting COVID-19? What changes did COVID-19 bring to your life and how did you handle them?

Information Repeating

Read the information below and repeat it to the class with details.

Long-term Sequela of COVID-19

Researchers from King's College London looked at whether infection with COVID-19 affected performance in two rounds of online cognitive testing that took place in 2021 and 2022. Data was collected from over 3,000 participants of the COVID Symptom Study Biobank study, across 12 tasks that tested memory, attention, reasoning, processing speed, and motor control.

The participants whose test scores were most affected by COVID-19 were those who had experienced symptoms related to the virus for 12 weeks or more. In these people, the effect of COVID-19 on test accuracy was comparable in size to the effect of a 10-year increase in age. There was no significant improvement in these test scores between the two rounds of testing, which took place nine months apart. By the second round of testing, the average time since participants' initial COVID-19 infection was almost two years.

Digging deeper into the analysis, the researchers separated participants by whether they felt fully recovered following COVID-19 infection. People who felt fully recovered after COVID-19 infection performed similarly to those who had not had the virus at all. In contrast, participants who did not feel fully recovered after infection had lower task accuracy scores on average.

Lead author Dr. Nathan Cheetham, a Senior Postdoctoral Data Scientist at King's College London said:

"Our findings suggest that, for people who were living with long-term symptoms after having COVID-19, the effects of the coronavirus on mental processes such as the ability to recall words and shapes are still detectable at an average of almost two years since their initial infection.

However, the result that COVID had no effect on performance in our tests for people who felt fully recovered, even if they'd had symptoms for several months and could be considered as experiencing 'long COVID', was good news. This study shows the need to monitor those people whose brain function is most affected by COVID-19, to see how their cognitive symptoms continue to develop and provide support towards recovery."

(Adapted from *sciencedaily.com*)

Interpretation

Interpret the following paragraphs into English with what you have learned in Part A.

Paragraph 1

现在越来越多的人饲养宠物，并和宠物产生大量互动，但是宠物身上常会携带一些传染病。除了被宠物咬伤或抓伤，有时仅仅是抚摸宠物或接触其粪便都会导致我们被感染。因此，在接触宠物时我们必须保持谨慎，确保宠物已接种相关疫苗。如果主人生病了，也要减少或避免与宠物接触，更不要与其分享食物，以防交叉传染。

Paragraph 2

一些不良生活习惯看似不起眼，但往往会引发或传播流行病。比如，挖鼻孔或咬指甲，这会将双手接触到的各种细菌和病毒带进鼻子或嘴巴，从而引发疾病。再比如，随地吐痰或擤鼻涕，这会把多种病原体带入空气中，造成飞沫传播。我们必须时刻注意个人卫生习惯，这既是防止流行病传播的办法，也是尊重他人的体现。

Paragraph 3

夏季天气炎热，食物不易储藏，一不小心就会腐烂变质。各类蚊虫、细菌和病毒都在快速繁殖，极易污染水源和食物。因此，夏季是很多流行病的高发季节，比如主要通过蚊虫叮咬来传播的登革热(dengue)。在夏季，我们要尽可能远离积水、污水、垃圾等蚊虫密集的地方，同时减少皮肤暴露，以防被其叮咬而感染疾病。

Paragraph 4

感染新冠病毒后最常见的后遗症之一就是嗅觉和味觉的丧失。作为人类重要的生理功能，嗅觉和味觉可以起到识别、警报的作用。嗅觉和味觉的丧失不仅会导致食欲衰退、影响营养摄入、威胁身体健康，还会对我们的精神状况产生不利影响。医生表示，这一症状一般在两周到一月内即可自行好转，因此不必过于担忧。

A6. Extension

Synonym Discrimination

Can you figure out the differences among the words below?

Group 1：suspect / susceptible / suspicious

Group 2：deteriorate / exacerbate / worsen

Group 3：impact / influence / effect

Extensive Reading

Major Epidemics of the Modern Era

For more than a century, countries have wrestled with how to improve international cooperation in the face of major outbreaks of infectious diseases. The COVID-19 pandemic, which brought the world to a near halt in 2020 and has killed nearly seven million people, underscores the urgency.

1899-1923: sixth cholera pandemic

A new outbreak of cholera, a bacterial infection contracted through the consumption of contaminated food and water, begins in India at the turn of the century. It's the latest wave of a disease that has caused pandemics intermittently since the early 1800s. The outbreak spreads to Russia, as well as to parts of the Middle East and North Africa, ultimately killing hundreds of thousands of people with particularly high death tolls in India and Russia. Advancements in sanitation and public hygiene are credited with preventing the pandemic from taking hold in Europe and North America.

1918-1920: Spanish Flu engulfs the globe

A new influenza virus begins to spread worldwide amid the upheavals of World War I. There is no consensus on the origin of the pandemic, but it is first publicly reported in Spain. It infects an estimated five hundred million people, roughly one-third of the world's population at the time, and kills some fifty million, with an unusually high fatality rate among otherwise healthy young adults. Many governments look to isolation measures, quarantines, and disinfecting efforts, but the global movement of troops hinders containment. At the time, there is no flu vaccine and antibiotics have not yet been developed to treat secondary bacterial infections. In the United States alone, about 675,000 people die, lowering the country's average life expectancy by more than twelve years.

1957-1958: Asian Flu pandemic

A new strain of influenza virus, designated H2N2, is reported in Singapore in February 1957, and soon spreads to China, the United Kingdom (UK), and the United States. Though less severe than the Spanish Flu, the Asian Flu kills more than one million people worldwide. A second wave of cases beginning at the end of that year is particularly deadly, and young children, elderly people, and pregnant women are hardest hit. A vaccine is quickly developed in 1957, but its deployment is limited and it does little to mitigate the outbreak, experts later say.

1961-Present: World's longest pandemic

A cholera pandemic originating in Indonesia spreads to other parts of Asia, the Middle East, and Africa over the course of a decade, and continues to this day. By the 1990s outbreaks also take hold in South America, the first on that continent in nearly a century. An outbreak in Zimbabwe in 2008-2009 kills more than four thousand people, and major outbreaks in Haiti and Yemen each affect more than a half million people. Some three million people are infected with the bacteria that cause cholera each year, and it remains endemic in close to fifty countries. Health experts say oral cholera vaccines, introduced in the 1990s, are not a replacement for improved sanitation.

1968-1969: Hong Kong Flu pandemic

A decade after the Asian Flu, a new strain called H3N2 emerges. Commonly called the Hong Kong Flu, it emerges first in Hong Kong in July 1968. It soon travels across East and South Asia, then to Australia, Europe, and North America, and on to Africa and South America by 1969. U.S. troops returning from the Vietnam War are believed to have brought the virus to the United States. An estimated one million people die in the pandemic, about half of them Hong Kong citizens and many of them people sixty-five years of age or older. Descendants of the H3N2 virus continue to circulate seasonally worldwide.

1977-1980: Smallpox eradicated

The last known case of smallpox, a viral disease that plagued humans for millennia, is diagnosed in 1977 in Somalia, following a nearly two-decade-long global vaccination campaign. Three years later the WHO formally declares it eradicated around the globe. The elimination of the disease, which was fatal in as many as one-third of patients, marks unusual U.S.-Soviet cooperation during the Cold War. It also highlights major advancements in the study and use of vaccines: polio vaccines introduced in the 1950s and 1960s lead to similar success globally, and vaccines are credited with reducing rates of illnesses such as measles, diphtheria, and whooping cough to all-time lows.

2002-2003: SARS emerges in China

The Severe Acute Respiratory Syndrome (SARS) coronavirus, part of a family of viruses that commonly cause respiratory symptoms such as coughing and shortness of breath, is first identified in late 2002 in southern China. SARS spreads to more than two dozen countries across four continents, infecting more than eight thousand people. In March 2003, the WHO triggers its Global Outbreak Alert and Response Network (GOARN) to coordinate research by teams of international experts and the deployment of supplies and health workers to affected countries. SARS kills close to eight hundred. The outbreak is quelled in mid-2003. The virus is thought to have been transmitted to humans via contact with civet cats.

2009-2010: U.S. at center of H1N1 pandemic

A new influenza virus, labeled H1N1 and commonly referred to as the swine flu because of its links to influenza viruses that circulate in pigs, begins to spread in early 2009 in Mexico and the United States. Unlike other strains of influenza, H1N1 disproportionately affects children and younger people. The Centers for Disease Control and Prevention (CDC) calls it the "first global flu pandemic in forty years". The WHO declares a PHEIC (Public Health Emergency of International Concern) in April 2009, then designates the spread of H1N1 a pandemic in June, after the virus reaches more than seventy countries. In response, some countries advise against travel to North America, and China imposes mandatory quarantines for patients and their close contacts. The CDC estimates that between 151,700 and 575,400 people die worldwide — around 12,500 in the United States — in the first year after the virus is discovered. Around 80 percent of those who die are younger than sixty-five. The WHO announces the pandemic's end in August 2010, though the strain continues to circulate seasonally.

2012: MERS uncovered in Middle East

A new coronavirus, named Middle East Respiratory Syndrome (MERS), is transmitted to humans from camels in 2012 in Saudi Arabia. The largest outbreak occurs on the Arabian Peninsula in the first half of 2014, with the Saudi city of Jeddah as its epicenter. In 2015, South Korea is home to the second-largest outbreak. More than two dozen countries report cases of the viral respiratory disease in the following years, though the majority of cases are in Saudi Arabia. The virus commonly causes pneumonia in those infected and has a relatively high fatality rate: of the roughly 2,500 people diagnosed with MERS since its discovery, more than 850 have died from the disease.

2014: uptick in polio prompts WHO emergency

In May 2014, WHO Director-General Margaret Chan declares a PHEIC over a rise in polio cases in Africa and Asia. The virus, which paralyzed or killed hundreds of thousands of people yearly at its peak, had been nearly eradicated after mass vaccination campaigns starting in the late 1950s. The disease, which disproportionately affects young people, proves hard to eliminate completely, particularly in conflict zones. Widespread mistrust of vaccination programs is a major challenge. As of 2022, the PHEIC over the possible spread of polio remains in place, and the disease is still endemic in Afghanistan and Pakistan.

2014-2016: Ebola sweeps West Africa

In early 2014, cases of the Ebola virus, a rare and severe infectious disease that leads to death in roughly half of those who contract it, are detected in Guinea and soon after in Liberia and Sierra Leone. It is the first time the disease moves into densely populated urban areas, allowing for rapid transmission. The outbreak eventually spreads to seven other countries, including several European states and the United States, causing more than eleven thousand deaths in all. Mistrust of health workers and rumors again present challenges to containment. The WHO, which declares the outbreak a PHEIC in August 2014, is criticized for what many call a slow response. In September 2014, the UN Security Council adopts a resolution calling on member states to pool global resources to combat the crisis, and countries including the United States and the UK deploy health workers and other aid. The hardest-hit countries declare themselves Ebola-free in June 2016.

2015: Fight against mosquito-borne diseases continues

The WHO reports in 2015 that malaria infections are down by more than one-third globally compared to 2000, as the United Nations and the Bill & Melinda Gates Foundation launch a major joint effort to eradicate the disease by 2040. Malaria still kills several hundred thousand people yearly, two-thirds of whom are children under five. Eradication efforts focus on the eleven countries where the large majority of malaria cases occur, all of which are in sub-Saharan Africa except for India. Meanwhile, cases of dengue, another mosquito-borne disease, spike between 2000 and 2015, partly due to increased reporting. Dengue is endemic in more than a hundred countries, with the majority of the 100-400 million yearly cases occurring in Asia. These diseases have proven difficult to eliminate, as researchers confront numerous challenges to developing successful vaccines.

2015-2016: Zika spreads across Americas

An outbreak of the Zika virus, first discovered in Uganda in the 1940s and transmitted mainly by mosquitoes, takes off in Brazil in early 2015. In February 2016, the WHO declares the outbreak a PHEIC, and by the middle of the year more than sixty countries report cases of the virus, including the United States. Thousands of women infected with the virus while pregnant give birth to babies with microcephaly, a condition in which a child's head is smaller than normal, and other congenital conditions. Some governments urge women to delay pregnancy amid the outbreak. Despite calls for cancellation, the 2016 Summer Olympics in Rio de Janeiro go ahead as planned. The WHO declares the end of the epidemic in November 2016.

2018-2020: Ebola returns in conflict-stricken Congo

In August 2018, the Democratic Republic of Congo (DRC) declares an outbreak of the Ebola virus in the country's northeast. Several cases are later reported across the border in Uganda. Protracted conflict in the area hampers the response, as health workers face attacks by armed groups; misinformation and mistrust among the local population are also challenges. By June 2019, the Ebola outbreak becomes the second largest in history, and in July the WHO declares a PHEIC, urging increased international support to end the crisis. More than 3,400 people are infected with the virus, and close to 2,300 die. In June 2020, nearly two years after the outbreak's start, the WHO declares it over. However, smaller outbreaks continue to crop up in parts of the country.

2019-2023: COVID-19 runs rampant

A new coronavirus emerges in China's Hubei Province in late 2019, spreading rapidly to other parts of China. The virus soon travels throughout the rest of the world, and in March 2020, the WHO designates the outbreak a PHEIC. Many governments impose restrictions to try to stop its spread, including lockdowns, mandates to wear face masks, limits on large gatherings, and quarantines for people who are infected. After three years, the official WHO death toll from the COVID-19 disease nears seven million people, though the actual number is believed to be up to three times higher. The economic decline is described as the worst since the Great Depression, with supply-chain and labor-force disruptions reverberating worldwide. At the same time, the world marks the fastest-ever development of safe and effective vaccines. However, uneven vaccine distribution and the emergence of more dangerous variants frustrate global efforts to end the pandemic. In May 2023, with 70 percent of the global population having at least one vaccine dose and a decline in COVID-19-related deaths and hospitalizations, the WHO director-general lifts the PHEIC, calling for a transition to long-term management of the pandemic.

2022-2023: A race to contain mpox

A case of mpox, formerly known as monkeypox, a rare zoonotic virus, is reported in the UK in May 2022. The virus is similar to smallpox, because it leads to some of the same symptoms and both are from the orthopoxvirus family. However, mpox is considered less transmissible and less fatal. The virus spreads rapidly in countries where it is not endemic; by July, there are around sixteen thousand reported cases and three confirmed deaths, and the disease is present in at least seventy-five countries. Because smallpox vaccines can be used to fight mpox, countries work to expand their limited availability. A rapid global response to the outbreak leads its spread to slow significantly by May 2023, with 87,000 reported cases and 140 confirmed deaths across 111 countries. That month, the WHO declares that mpox is no longer a public health emergency.

(Adapted from *cfr.org*)

Part B Prevention and Control

B1. Introduction

How to Prevent Infections

Infections are caused by microscopic organisms known as pathogens, the bacteria, viruses, fungi, or parasites that enter the body, multiply, and interfere with normal functions. Infectious diseases are a leading cause of illness and death around the world. For certain people, particularly those with underlying illnesses like heart disease or cancer, those who have serious injuries, or those who are taking medications that weaken the immune system, it's more difficult to avoid getting sick with an infection. Living in a modern society, the threat we face from deadly viruses, bacteria, and parasites can seem remote, but these infectious microbes are ever present among us. However, for most healthy people, following a few basic principles can go a long way in helping to prevent infections.

Understanding how infections are transmitted can help you avoid getting sick

Not long ago, no one understood that infectious diseases were caused by tiny organisms that moved from person to person. Even now, although we know that microscopic living microbes cause disease, how they do so is not always obvious. But we do know that most microbes enter through openings in the body, our noses, mouths, ears, cuts on the skin, and genital passages. They can also be transmitted through our skin through insect or animal bites. The best way to prevent infections is to block pathogens from entering the body.

Good hygiene: the primary way to prevent infections

The first line of defense is to keep germs at bay by following good personal hygiene habits. Prevent infection before it begins and avoid spreading it to others with these easy measures.

- Remember to wash your hands. Besides washing your hands after using the bathroom, before preparing or eating food, and after gardening or other dirty tasks. You should also wash up after blowing your nose, coughing, or sneezing; feeding or stroking your pet; or visiting or caring for a sick person.
- Cover a cough. Cover your mouth and nose with a tissue when you sneeze or cough,

then dispose of it. If no tissue is handy, cough or sneeze into your elbow rather than into your hands.

- Wash and bandage all cuts. Any serious cut or animal or human bite should be examined by a doctor.
- Do not pick at healing wounds or blemishes, or squeeze pimples.
- Don't share dishes, glasses, or eating utensils.
- Avoid direct contact with napkins, tissues, handkerchiefs, or similar items used by others.

Practice good food-safety techniques to avoid getting sick

Although most cases of food-borne infection are not dangerous, some can lead to serious medical conditions, including kidney failure and meningitis. You can prevent infections by food-borne pathogens in your household by preparing and storing foods safely. The following precautions will help kill microbes that are present in the food you buy and help you avoid introducing new microbes into your food at home.

- Rinse all meat, poultry, fish, fruits, and vegetables under running water before cooking or serving them.
- Wash your hands with soap and water before and after you handle raw meat.
- Separate raw foods and cooked foods. Don't use the same utensils or cutting boards with cooked meat that were used to prepare the raw meat without washing between uses.
- Cook foods thoroughly, using a meat thermometer to ensure that whole poultry is cooked to 180°F (about 82.2°C), roasts and steaks to 145°F (about 63°C), and ground meats to 160°F (about 71°C).
- Defrost foods only in the refrigerator or in the microwave.

Vaccinations are essential if you are to avoid getting sick

Whether you are young or young at heart, getting vaccinated is an essential part of staying healthy. Many serious infections can be prevented by immunization. While vaccines may cause some common side effects, such as a temporarily sore arm or low fever, they are generally safe and effective.

- Children should receive the recommended childhood vaccinations.
- Adults should make sure their vaccinations are up to date.
- When traveling abroad, check with your health care provider about additional immunizations.
- Make sure your pet's vaccinations are up to date, too. In addition to protecting your

pet, this will also protect you and your family.

Take travel precautions

If you are planning a trip, ask your doctor if you need any immunizations. Discuss your travel plans with your physician at least three months before you leave.

- Get your shots before you leave your country. Avoid getting any unnecessary shots, immunizations, or tattoos abroad.
- Do not consume ice while traveling. Freezing does not kill all water-borne infectious microbes.
- Drink only bottled drinks, such as soft drinks or bottled water that have secure caps. Be aware that some fruit juices may be made with impure local water.
- Do not eat fruit you haven't peeled yourself, or consume dairy products (milk may not be pasteurized).

(Adapted from *health.harvard.edu*)

B2. Words and Expressions

Vocabulary

1. antipyretic /ˌæntɪpaɪˈretɪk/ *n.* 退烧药
2. utensil /juːˈtensɪl/ *n.* (尤指厨房或家用的)器具,用具
3. emollient /ɪˈmɑːliənt/ *n.* 润肤剂,护肤霜
4. sanitize /ˈsænətaɪz/ *v.* 给……消毒;对……进行卫生处理
5. detergent /dɪˈtɜːdʒənt/ *n.* 清洁剂;洗衣液
6. filter /ˈfɪltə/ *n.&v.* 过滤(器)
7. repellent /rɪˈpelənt/ *n.* 驱虫剂
8. disposable /dɪˈspəʊzəbəl/ *adj.* 一次性的,用后可扔掉的
9. ventilation /ˌventəlˈeɪʃən/ *n.* 通风(设备);空气流通(设备)
10. electrolyte /ɪˈlektrəlaɪt/ *n.* 电解质;(通常指)电解液

Must-haves	**必备物品**
soap	肥皂
alcohol-based hand rub	含酒精的洗手液

alcohol spray	酒精喷雾
facial tissue	面巾纸
toilet roll / toilet paper	卫生纸
wet wipe	湿巾
cooling patches	退烧贴
hand sanitizer	消毒洗手液
facial mask	口罩
disposable tissue	一次性纸巾
antiseptics	抗菌剂;消毒防腐剂
emollient	润肤剂,护肤霜
eating utensils	餐具
towel	毛巾
separate bedding	单独的床品
disinfectant	消毒剂
Q-tips	棉签
water filter	水过滤器
water purifier	净水器
air purifier	空气净化器
sanitary ware	卫生洁具
ventilation system	新风系统
airtight bag	密封袋
gloves	手套
infrared thermometer	红外测温仪
antigen test kit	抗原试剂盒
iodine	碘;碘酒
saline solution	生理盐水
vitamin tablets	维生素片
dietary supplement	营养补充剂
electrolyte replenishment beverage	电解质补充饮料
antipyretic	退烧药
antiviral drug	抗病毒药
anti-inflammatory	抗炎的;消炎药
anti-diarrhoeal	止泻药
detergent	清洁剂;洗衣液

pesticide	杀虫剂
mosquito repellent	驱蚊剂

Vocabulary

1. regimen /ˈredʒəmən/ *n.* 养生之道
2. metabolism /məˈtæbəlɪzəm/ *n.* 新陈代谢
3. scrub /skrʌb/ *v.* (用硬刷、肥皂和水)擦洗,刷洗
4. psychotherapy /ˌsaɪkəʊˈθerəpi/ *n.* 心理疗法,精神疗法
5. disinfect /dɪsɪnˈfekt/ *v.* 消毒;除去(感染)
6. etiquette /ˈetɪkɪt/ *n.* 礼仪,礼节;规范,规则
7. vigilant/ˈvɪdʒələnt/ *adj.* 警觉的;警戒的;警惕的
8. ambient /ˈæmbɪənt/ *adj.* 周围的;(尤指)周围环境条件的
9. immaculately /ɪˈmækjələtli/ *adv.* 洁净地;完好地
10. dedicated /ˈdedəkeɪtɪd/ *adj.* 专用的;尽心尽力的,尽职尽责

Prevention and Control Measures	**防控措施**
non-pharmaceutical interventions (NPI)	非药物干预措施
large gathering cancellation	禁止大规模聚会
travel restriction	旅行限制
quarantine	自我隔离,定点隔离
mandatory isolation	强制医疗隔离
voluntary vaccination	自愿疫苗接种
food recalls	食品召回
public messaging and education	公共信息与教育
biosafety	生物安全
work from home	在家工作
a dedicated bathroom	专用卫生间
health monitoring	健康监测
hand hygiene	手部卫生
air dry thoroughly	彻底风干
rinse off with clean water	用清水冲洗

scrub off the muck	用力擦洗掉污物
stay home when sick	生病时待在家里
completely cover one's nose and mouth	完全遮住抠鼻
stay up-to-date with vaccinations	及时接种疫苗
limit alcohol intake	限制酒精摄入量
use separate dishes	使用单独的餐具
replace the bedding regularly	定期更换床品
ventilate the room	让房间通风
ambient temperature	环境温度;周围温度
deworm	驱虫
serving chopsticks and spoon	公筷和公勺
individually served meals	分餐制
take a daily shower	每天洗澡
eat healthy and balanced meals	饮食健康均衡
maintain good hygiene	保持良好的卫生习惯
regular handwashing	经常洗手
stay away from wild or pet rodents	远离野生或宠物啮齿动物
regular checkups for pets	宠物定期体检
shower after swimming	游泳后淋浴
pay attention to water quality	留心水质
clean contact lenses	清洁隐形眼镜
disinfect regularly	定期消毒
handle the food carefully	小心处理食物
refrigerate promptly	及时冷藏
store food in sealed containers	用密封容器储存食物
use separate cutting boards	使用单独的砧板
defrost food in the microwave	用微波炉解冻食物
keep countertops immaculately clean	保持(厨房)台面干净整洁
limit nonessential meetings	限制非必要会议
limit visitors	限制访客
distance learning	远程学习
avoid reusing single-use masks	避免重复使用一次性口罩
discard after use	用后丢弃
non-food contact surface	非食物接触面

personal grooming	个人仪容;个人卫生
be more physically active	加强体育锻炼
get good sleep	保持良好的睡眠
improve one's metabolism	改善新陈代谢
keep social distance	保持社交距离
practice cough etiquette	践行咳嗽礼仪(如咳嗽时捂住口、鼻等)
flexed elbow	屈肘
get some sunlight exposure	晒太阳
set up a good regimen	建立良好的养生之道
avoid being neglectful and careless	避免粗心大意
remain vigilant	保持警惕
stay calm and positive	保持冷静和乐观
accept the psychotherapy	接受心理治疗
separate labor room	隔离分娩室
interruption of mother-to-infant transmission	母婴阻断
newborn follow-up	新生儿随访

Vocabulary

1. vaccination /ˌvæksɪˈneɪʃn/ *n*. 接种疫苗,种痘
2. candidate /ˈkændɪdeɪt/ *n*. 候选,候补者
3. efficacious /ˌefɪˈkeɪʃəs/ *adj*. 有效的;灵验的
4. caveat /ˈkævɪæt/ *n*. (进一步行动前的)警告,告诫
5. prioritize /praɪˈɒrətaɪz/ *v*. 按优先顺序列出;优先处理,优先考虑
6. contraindication /ˌkɑːntrəɪndəˈkeɪʃən/ *n*. (对某种药物或疗法的)禁忌症
7. preservative /prɪˈzɜːvətɪv/ *n*. 防腐剂,保护剂
8. amoxicillin /əˈmɒksəsɪlɪn/ *n*. 阿莫西林
9. penicillins /ˌpenəˈsɪlɪn/ *n*. 盘尼西林,青霉素
10. cephalosporin /ˌsefəˈlɒspɒrɪn/ *n*. 头孢菌素

Vaccination	**疫苗接种**
candidate vaccine / vaccine candidates	候选疫苗
human trial	人体试验
inoculation	预防接种，预防注射
safe and efficacious	安全有效
laboratory animal	实验动物，试验动物
clinical trials	临床试验
the intended prioritized populations	预定的优先人群
inactivated vaccine	灭活疫苗；灭能疫苗
dose	一剂；剂量
booster	辅助药剂，加强药剂，加强针
mild side effects	轻微的副作用
moderate	温和的，适度的
immune cells	免疫细胞
low-grade fever	低热
adverse effect	不利影响，副作用
preservatives	防腐剂；保鲜剂
concentration	浓度
mass vaccination campaign	大规模预防接种
vaccination caveats	接种注意事项
sign the informed consent	签署知情同意书
a watch note	留观条
observation period	观察期
abnormal condition	异常情况
local redness and pain	局部红肿
interval	时间间隔
shot site	接种部位
vaccine ingredient	疫苗成分
vaccination record	接种记录
contraindication	禁忌症候
underlying health conditions	潜在的健康状况
an acute episode	急性发作期
anaphylaxis	过敏性
amoxicillin	阿莫西林

cephalosporin	头孢菌素
penicillins	青霉素类
pregnant and lactating women	孕妇和哺乳期妇女
pregnancy	孕期
delayed vaccination	延后接种

Vocabulary

1. expenditure /ɪk'spendətʃə/ *n.* (政府或个人的)全部开支,花费
2. nebulizer /'nebjəlaɪzə/ *n.* 雾化器,喷鼻器
3. anteroom /'æntɪruːm/ *n.* 缓冲间;接待室,前厅
4. dietitian /ˌdaɪə'tɪʃən/ *n.* 营养保健专家,营养学家,营养师
5. orderly /'ɔːrdəli/ *n.* (医院的)护工,勤杂工
6. auxiliary /ɑːg'zɪləri/ *adj.* & *n.* 辅助的;辅助人员
7. obstetrician /ˌɑːbstə'trɪʃən/ *n.* 产科医生
8. anesthesiologist /ˌænəsˌθiːzi'ɑːlədʒɪst/ *n.* 麻醉师
9. gurney /'gɜːni/ *n.* (医院中推送病人用的)轮床
10. consultation /ˌkɑːnsʌl'teɪʃən/ *n.* 协商会;咨询会;会诊;咨询

Hospitalization	**住院治疗**
out-of-pocket medical expenditure	自费医疗支出
medical insurance card	医保卡
medical supplies	医疗物资
googles	护目镜
face shield	面罩
surgical gown	手术衣
protective suit	防护服
N95 respirator	N95 口罩
surgical mask	医用外科口罩
medical isolation shoe covers	医用隔离鞋套
surgical cap	手术帽
surgical drape	手术巾

nebulizer	雾化器,喷鼻器
pacemaker	心脏起搏器
electrocardiogram monitor	心电监护仪
oxygenerator	制氧机
pulse oximeter	血氧仪
nurse's station	护士站
operation room	手术室
waiting room	候诊室
birthing / delivery room	产房
emergency room (ER)	急诊室
Intensive Care Unit (ICU)	重症监护室
clinic reception	分诊台
anteroom	缓冲间
dietitian	营养师
orderly	护理员
nurse's aide / auxiliary nurse	护工,助理护士
surgeon	外科医生
surgical nurse	外科护士
anesthesiologist	麻醉师
obstetrician	产科医生
midwife / nurse-midwife	助产护士
emergency medical technician (EMT)	急诊技师;急救医务人员
radiology department	放射科
X-ray technician	X 光技师
lab-technician	实验室技术员
radiologist	放射科医生
intensivist	重症特护医生
hospital bed capacity	医院病床数量
normal ward	普通病房
private ward	私人病房
cohorting	集中照护
hospital gown	病号服
hospital bed	病床
bed control	病床调节器

call button	呼叫按钮
vital signs monitor	生命体征监视器
bed table	床上用餐桌
bed pan	床上用便盆
gurney	轮床
medical history form	病历表
medical chart	医疗信息表
electrocardiogram (ECG)	心电图
ward round	查房
consultation	会诊
hospital course	住院治疗情况
discharge instructions	出院医嘱
discharge medications	出院后用药

B3. Situational Conversations

Conversation 1 Talking about the Role of Social Media Related to COVID-19

V: Varga P: Ed Pertwee

V: As you know, **vaccine hesitancy** is presenting a growing challenge for countries seeking to close the immunization gap. Regarding vaccination, do social media play a role in influencing vaccination uptake and vaccine safety concerns?

P: The available evidence suggests that digital media do play a role in influencing people's attitudes towards vaccines, but it's difficult to quantify the scale of the effect because there are so many other factors at play. Some academic studies have used experimental designs to try to control this, but we need to be careful about how we **interpret** these, as experimental settings can never precisely **mimic** the real-world contexts in which people consume digital content.

One key finding across a number of different studies is that in terms of the relationship between social media and vaccine hesitancy, the problem seems to be informational reliance on social media, not social media usage **per se**. In other words, the issue is not how much you use social media, or how often you encounter misinformation there, but the extent to which you come to rely on social media as a sole or main source of information about vaccines.

V: Do you think those social media have responsibility in tackling the spread of misinformation on their platforms?

P: Social media platforms do have a responsibility to address the spread of misinformation and other harmful content on their platforms. At the very least, they need to ensure that their recommendation algorithms (推荐算法) are not promoting such content and that they are not profiting from it.

V: That's true. I read that an investigation by a UK-based campaign group early in the COVID pandemic estimated that English-language anti-vaccination accounts alone could be worth up to nearly 1 billion euros to the platforms, a huge sum of money. That's horrifying. So, in your opinion, should other communicational tools, such as **SMS** or voice calls, be used to disseminate adequate information related to vaccination?

P: Of course. Some emerging findings and studies all suggest that communicational tools may have a role to play in supplementing other forms of vaccine communication, for example during crisis situations where healthcare systems are **overwhelmed** and it's difficult to get a face-to-face appointment with a healthcare provider.

(Adapted from *sciencemediahub.eu*)

☞ **Notes**

- **vaccine hesitancy:** a delay in acceptance, or refusal, of vaccines despite the availability of vaccine services and supporting evidence.
- **interpret:** to explain the meaning of something; or to translate, especially oral remarks.
- **mimic:** to copy the way in which a particular person usually speaks and moves, usually in order to make people laugh.
- **per se:** by or of itself.
- **SMS:** an abbreviation of Short Message / Messaging Service.
- **overwhelmed:** be too much for someone or something to manage.

Conversation 2 An Interview with Dr. Sabine Franklin

I: Interviewer F: Dr. Franklin

I: Franklin, please first tell us a little bit about your work in the countries of West Africa that were affected by Ebola.

F: The three main countries that were affected by the Ebola virus disease during the 2014-2016 outbreak are Guinea, Liberia, and Sierra Leone, and they were in a state of recovery from the civil wars. A lot of their infrastructure had been destroyed. When we think about infrastructure, we're talking about money, people, and things. The roads were pretty much destroyed. Buildings, hospitals, schools were burned down during the war time, as well as people fled or were displaced. And this region is also where Ebola started in 2014. It's actually not quite a **coincidence** that Ebola kind of came out from this area, if we think about the virus being very rural dominant. And there's also a lack of health care infrastructure, so people were very sick.

I: So what were you looking at when you went there?

F: When I visited Sierra Leone the first time after Ebola, like right after I interviewed a range of different people, healthcare professionals, government workers, NGO workers, and the traditional leaders and community leaders. They passed the bylaws, which acted as emergency management regulations. So things that, believe it or not, we are familiar with today with COVID, such as stay-at-home orders, banning gatherings. They **mandated healthcare referrals** and that really helped with the Ebola virus disease outbreak, because by mandating healthcare referrals, they encouraged people to seek treatment earlier.

I: In your ongoing research on outbreaks, you found that people don't always apply lessons learned to diseases, like what we've seen in the COVID-19 pandemic. Now we have a new threat, H5N1 bird flu. It's not new. It's been around for 20 years, but you've been watching how the world's responding to the renewed spread of this virus. Tell us what we haven't learned on a global level.

F: H5N1, as you said, we have been warned about for nearly 20 years, but the policy of **culling** birds and **poultry** has been in place for many years as well. But the avian flu has kept recurring. So if culling birds in prior outbreaks had worked, we would not be having a recurrence of avian flu pandemic. Not only did this practice not work, and we keep having outbreaks, but now we're seeing it in different species of mammals that are infected and dying from the virus. We need to change course, because culling mammals is not going to work either, right?

I think that we as a society, we need to change our perspectives on disease outbreaks, whether it is bird flu or Ebola. We're not going to be able to solve every disease with a pill or rapid vaccine development. We need to reconsider how we interact with the environment and animals, and that means adjusting urbanization policies, stronger environmental protection, and taking a look at the practice of mass agricultural farming.

Basically these are going to change much of the way that we live, where currently, anything and everything is conveniently available for our consumption, because these things impact planetary health, which in turn will impact animal and human health. So we must advocate for governments to restructure their economies and societies to balance our wants with what the planet needs.

I: Franklin, thank you so much for joining us.

F: Thank you again for inviting me. It was a real pleasure to speak with you.

(Adapted from *onehealthtrust.org*)

☞ **Notes**

- **healthcare referral:** a written request from one health professional to another health professional or health service, asking them to diagnose or treat the patient for a particular condition.
- **coincidence:** an occasion when two or more similar things happen at the same time, especially in a way that is unlikely and surprising.
- **mandate:** to give official permission for something to happen.
- **cull:** to reduce the size of (a herd or flock) by killing a proportion of its members.
- **poultry:** domestic fowls raised for meat or eggs; chickens, turkeys, ducks, geese, etc. collectively.

Conversation 3 An Interview with Amanda McClelland

I: Interviewer A: Amanda McClelland

I: You work to prevent epidemics. So, the world knows a lot about how to prevent cholera, but it's popping up again everywhere. How can that be?

A: It's surprising we think about cholera as one of those old diseases that we've overcome. It has been about 170 years since **John Snow** first found the water sources in London and found out whether they're the cause of cholera. But we have more than 25 countries currently suffering an outbreak at the moment; it is really exploding. And it's a combination of things.

I think, in part, fatigue coming out of COVID when health systems were disrupted. Healthcare workers were very focused on COVID and cholera took the opportunity. And we've also had a large number of natural disasters and conflicts that really drive cholera.

I: Now, clean water is the first step to preventing cholera spread. Why is it so difficult to manage this issue of clean water?

A: Yeah, it's one of those difficult questions that we need to overcome. Everyone deserves clean water. We have multiple ways to get clean water for people but there's still millions of people around the globe that don't have access to clean water every day. But what's driving the cholera outbreaks is those natural disasters that contaminated the water. The drought makes water sources more difficult to access. And so, it's really about what access and water quality are really being impacted by climate change and a number of these large natural disasters.

I: What can we learn from the cholera response that can help us prepare better to fight other outbreaks?

A: It's a really good question. And I think from my experience, cholera is the perfect response to build capacity. You need all of the skills in terms of collaborating, good engagement with community. You need behavior change. You need to explain how cholera has spread. Basic things like boiling water, or accessing safe water, using **latrines**, or washing hands are all things that can stop the outbreak, as well as good epidemiology and following the data. So, if you can get good at cholera outbreaks, it's very transferable to other outbreaks. We are supposed to use this opportunity to build our capacity back up. Make sure that we have enough people trained across the world in epidemiology, in their behavior change, communication, and case management. Building up that capacity again that's been so depleted post-COVID is not just to tackle these cholera outbreaks, but also to make sure that we're better prepared for others.

I: So, what do you recommend that the world do to stop all of these cholera outbreaks from popping up?

A: It needs a **multipronged** approach. I think the WHO has just called for more support, so there's definitely a financing issue. The world is also fatigued after COVID. The lack of sustained funding to be able to tackle outbreaks, especially these types of outbreaks that can be isolated in poorer communities are really important. So we need the right supplies and the right level of support for response. We need access to more vaccines, but also more access to supplies. We need to make sure that we're following the data and getting all the way to the end. But we also need better prevention and preparedness. Many of these outbreaks have come on the back of natural disasters because health systems have been damaged because of flooding and challenges in clean and safe water. So, it really is that holistic approach to making sure that people have access to basic services, even during natural disasters, and restrengthening the health system to be able to detect and respond quickly.

(Adapted from *onehealthtrust.org*)

☞**Notes**

- **John Sown:** an English physician and a leader in the development of anesthesia and medical hygiene. He is considered one of the founders of modern epidemiology, in part because of his work in tracing the source of a cholera outbreak in Soho, London, in 1854.
- **latrine:** a toilet or something used as a toilet or the use of a large number of people, as in an army camp.
- **multipronged:** having several distinct aspects or elements.

B4. Picture Knowledge

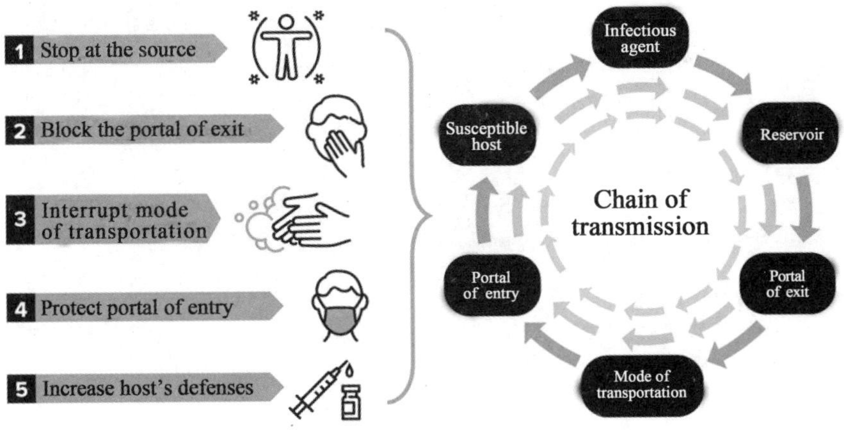

Pic. 2-3 5 steps of infection prevention

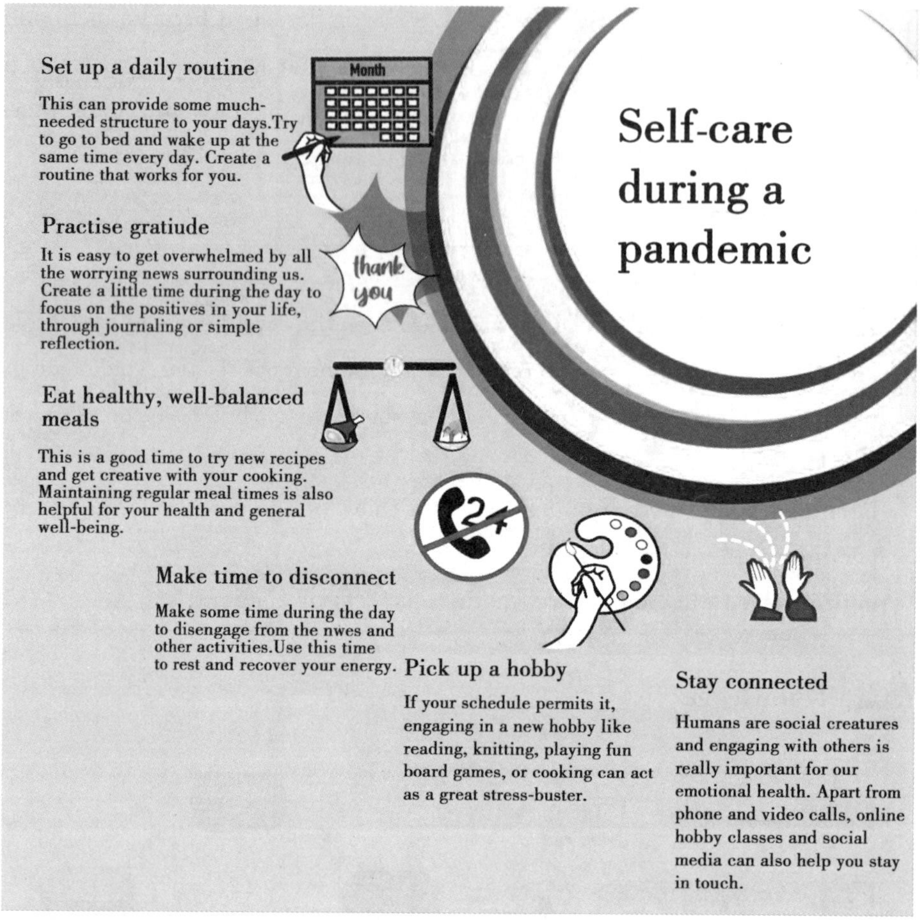

Pic. 2-4 Self-care during a pandemic

B5. Follow-up Activities

Discussion

University campuses are usually densely populated, and we all study, live and eat together, while sharing lots of items on our campus. In this environment, infectious diseases can spread very fast. What can we do to prevent the transmission of infectious diseases and protect ourselves on campus? You are suggested to use the expressions you have learned in this unit to share your tips.

Reading and Sharing

The following is an excerpt from the video message by United Nations High Commissioner for Human Rights at the Science and Technology in Society forum session "Shaping a post-COVID society".

> *"As individuals and societies, COVID-19 has highlighted our profound dependence on science and technology.*
>
> *For billions of people, digital technologies have meant studying and working from home; running businesses remotely; accessing essential information through online news outlets, government services and social media; staying in touch with family, loved ones and the entire outside world during lockdowns.*
>
> *These technologies are also essential for tackling the virus itself. Digital contact tracing is being used in many countries; tele-medicine increased the reach of healthcare; and artificial intelligence may be a strong asset in development of treatments and vaccines.*
>
> *...Everyone must have access to information, medicines and tools to prevent, detect and treat COVID-19, including a vaccine. The benefits of scientific progress, especially as they apply to life-saving innovations, are meant to be shared. At no time has this goal been more urgent."*

Conduct a group discussion on the following topics:

- Besides the benefits brought by technologies that have been talked above, what other changes have technologies made in our daily lives during the COVID-19 pandemic?
- From your own perspective, has COVID-19 contributed to the development of technologies and why?
- What can we do to make more people benefit from scientific progress in terms of epidemic prevention?

Information Repeating

Read the information below and repeat it to the class with details.

Getting a Good Night's Sleep Could Boost Your Response to Vaccination

We all know how important sleep is for mental health, but a meta-analysis publishing in the journal *Current Biology* on March 13, 2023, found that getting good shut-eye also helps our immune systems respond to vaccination. The authors found that people who slept less than six hours per night produced significantly fewer antibodies than people who slept seven hours or more, and the deficit was equivalent to two months of antibody waning.

"Good sleep not only amplifies but may also extend the duration of protection of the vaccine," says senior author Eve Van Cauter, professor emeritus at the University of Chicago who, along with lead author Karine Spiegel at the French National Institute of Health and Medicine, published a landmark study on the effects of sleep on vaccination in 2002. When the COVID-19 pandemic hit, and mass-vaccination became an international priority, Spiegel and Van Cauter set out to summarize our current knowledge about the effect of sleep duration on vaccine response.

To do this, they combed the literature and then combined and re-analyzed the results of seven studies that vaccinated for viral infections (influenza and hepatitis A and B). In their analysis, the team compared the antibody response for individuals who slept a "normal" amount (7-9 hours, as per the National Sleep Foundation's recommendation for healthy adults) with "short sleepers" who slept less than 6 hours per night. They compared the effect for men versus women and adults over the age of 65 years versus younger adults. Overall, they found strong evidence that sleeping less than 6 hours per night reduces the immune response to vaccination. When they analyzed men and women separately, though, the result was only significant in men, and the effect of sleep duration on antibody production was much more variable in women. This difference is probably due to fluctuating sex hormone levels in women, the authors say.

However, there's a lot more to be known about sleep and vaccination, the authors say. "We need to understand the sex differences, which days around the time of vaccination are most important, and exactly how much sleep is needed so that we can give guidance to people," says Spiegel. "We are going to be vaccinating millions and millions of people in the next few years, and this is an aspect that can help maximize protection."

(Adapted from *sciencedaily.com*)

Interpretation

Interpret the following paragraphs into English with what you have learned in Part B.

Paragraph 1

平常外出聚餐或者在家吃饭时，我们习惯于边聊边吃。出于习惯或"礼貌"而不使用公筷，或是用自己的筷子相互帮忙夹菜。这样的"亲密接触"其实是以我们的健康隐患为代价的，因为细菌、病毒都可以通过餐桌、筷子和飞沫进行传播。因此，践行良好的就餐礼仪是极有必要的，比如餐前餐后洗手，尽量使用公筷、公勺，实行分餐制等。为了更健康的生活，改变一下饮食习惯只是我们要付出的微小代价。

Paragraph 2

面对潜在的流行病危机，预防比治疗更重要。在日常生活中，我们必须注意保持良好的卫生习惯。在家中，我们要保持室内良好的通风，定期消毒常用物品。外出时，我们要避免共用个人物品，尽量佩戴口罩。我们要早睡早起，加强体育锻炼，保证充足的睡眠和健康均衡的饮食，还要注意勤洗手、保持社交距离、注射疫苗等，这些都是我们预防流行病的好方法。

Paragraph 3

众所周知，按时、全程、科学接种疫苗可以有效抵御疾病。接种前，我们需要了解接种疫苗的注意事项，确保自己不会对某些疫苗成分过敏或是产生强烈的副作用。接种当日，我们要保持注射部位清洁干燥，并注意个人卫生。接种后，我们还要在接种现场留观 30 分钟，密切观察自己的身体情况。如有任何不适，马上告知现场的医护人员。在接种后一周内，我们也要避免吃一些辛辣刺激或海鲜类食物，要多喝水，适当休息。

B6. Extension

Synonym Discrimination

Can you figure out the differences among the words below?

Group 1: clean / rinse / scrub

Group 2: handle / address / tackle

Group 3: isolation / quarantine / lockdown

Extensive Reading

Passage One

What Is "Disease X" and Should We Be Worried?

David Bass

"Disease X" is a name for an illness caused by a presently unknown, yet serious microbial threat. The idea is for society to be ready to rapidly and effectively respond to any as yet unknown disease that may arise to seriously threaten human health.

By getting scientists to work on medical countermeasures for unknown threats, not just known ones, it is hoped that vaccines, tests, and therapies can be rapidly deployed in the advent of any new COVID-style pandemic.

The term, Disease X, was coined by the World Health Organization (WHO) and put on their list of priority diseases. It is intended to focus research on entire classes of viruses, rather than individual strains. In a 2022 statement on the subject, the WHO defined the term: "Disease X is used to indicate an unknown pathogen that could cause a serious international epidemic."

Should we be worried?

It is important to remember that the term Disease X does not refer to any specific disease, rather it is a hypothetical concept of an as-yet-unknown disease that could arise in the future and turn into the next pandemic.

Unfortunately, the possibility of another COVID-19-style pandemic breaking out in the future is high. The changing state of the world that we live in could certainly generate another pandemic.

Thomas Russo, infectious diseases expert at the University of Buffalo Jacobs School of Medicine and Biomedical Sciences explains: "As mankind breaks down these barriers through live animal markets and deforestation, we need continued surveillance and studies and improved biosecurity across the world."

Disease X and climate change

"Over half of known human pathogenic diseases can be aggravated by climate change," a report, published in August 2022 by the international weekly scientific journal *Nature*, pointed out. "We found that 58% (that is, 218 out of 375) of infectious diseases confronted by humanity worldwide have been at some point aggravated by climatic hazards."

There are several ways in which climate change can impact disease. With the flooding predicted by the rising sea levels due to the melting of the polar ice caps, we can expect not only flooding but also waterborne diseases. Global warming could also cause defrosting of the tundra releasing many pathogens that could prove deadly.

Mass migration from overheated areas could lead to the spread of new pathogens while refugee camps that are likely to be set up are notorious for being breeding grounds for disease.

As temperatures rise and more areas become uninhabitable, animals and humans could be forced together in close quarters, increasing the likelihood of a disease jumping from one species to another. Warmer weather also means that there could be an increase in pests such as mosquitoes or ticks that carry infectious diseases.

Warmer oceanic conditions could also lead to deadly algae blooms that not only pose a threat to marine life but could generate diseases harmful to humans too.

Finally, climate change could affect the human immune system itself. Hotter conditions put more strain on the immune system and heatwaves could generate diseases that are resistant to them.

What can be done to prevent the Disease X's of the future?

Research and funding is being poured into preventing the pandemics of the future. There will be a new World Health Organization Hub for Pandemic and Epidemic Intelligence in Berlin. This is a five billion dollar US initiative to develop new vaccines and treatments for COVID-19, named Project NextGen.

There will also be $262.5 million in funding for a US network dedicated to detecting and responding to public health emergencies (such as Disease X-style pandemics).

Another project, called the Global Virome Project, aims to stop threats from animal diseases jumping species. And there's also the new World Bank-approved fund for pandemic prevention, preparedness and response.

(Adapted from *impakter.com*)

Passage Two

Vaccine Hesitancy Is One of the Greatest Threats to Global Health and the Pandemic Has Made It Worse

Simon Nicholas Williams

The COVID pandemic has disrupted many areas of routine healthcare including, importantly, childhood vaccination. The pandemic saw levels of essential childhood immunizations decline in more than 100 countries around the world, leading to outbreaks of infectious diseases such as yellow fever, cholera, diphtheria, and polio. There are many reasons for this, including issues with supply, restricted access to services, and in some areas, factors unrelated to the pandemic such as conflict. But one contributor that's important to recognize and address is vaccine hesitancy.

A perfect storm for infectious diseases

While COVID has had significant consequences for global vaccination rates, there are signs that, in some countries and for some diseases, there has been a longer-standing stalling or even decline in vaccine coverage. In England, for example, childhood vaccination coverage generally plateaued from around 2011 and declined from around 2014.

Rates of many infectious diseases declined at the height of the pandemic due to widespread social distancing measures, but cases have since started to increase. For example, the number of countries with significant measles outbreaks rose by 50% between 2020-2021 and 2022-2023. Cases have also recently occurred in some high-income countries with historically good vaccine coverage.

The combination of reduced vaccine coverage, overstretched healthcare systems, and the return to pre-pandemic levels of social contact have created a perfect storm for infectious disease rates to rise. Growing vaccine hesitancy is only likely to make this issue worse.

What drives vaccine hesitancy?

One of the main factors leading to hesitancy towards COVID vaccines specifically has been concern that the vaccines were developed too quickly. However, we know that COVID vaccines are safe and effective.

In our research on attitudes to COVID vaccines, my colleagues and I found that concerns over side-effects, distrust in government and a belief in conspiracy theories all increased hesitancy. And hesitancy around COVID shots could also lead to hesitancy "spillover" for other vaccines. The UNICEF (the United Nations International Children's Emergency Fund) report similarly notes that reduced trust in authorities, as well as the proliferation of misinformation and conspiracy theories on social media, are growing challenges to public perceptions of vaccines.

How do we increase vaccine confidence?

Vaccinations prevent 4 million to 5 million deaths a year. But according to the WHO, a further 1.5 million deaths could be avoided if global coverage of vaccinations improved. Reducing vaccine hesitancy is one part of the solution.

To address vaccine hesitancy, we need to tackle the root causes. We can look to the "three Cs model", which suggests we need to maximize convenience (making vaccines easy to access) and minimize complacency by adequately communicating the risks of diseases. The third "C" is confidence. Crucially, to increase confidence, we need to combat vaccine hesitancy caused by misinformation. One way to do this is through "inoculation" or "prebunking", where people are exposed to small amounts of false information—for example, in online games or social media videos. This helps bolster their "immunity" to misinformation by enhancing their critical assessment skills.

Another way is to use social media to combat misinformation by investing in the promotion of accurate information. Organizations such as the WHO and UNICEF will play a key role in building confidence globally.

In short, alongside efforts to catch kids up with vaccine doses missed during the pandemic, we also need to tackle misinformation. Otherwise, vaccine hesitancy will remain one of the greatest threats to global health for years to come.

(Adapted from *theconversation.com*)

Sources of Pictures

Pic. 2-1 Retrieved from *mdpi.com*

Pic. 2-2 Retrieved from *ottawapublichealth.ca*

Pic. 2-3 Retrieved from *uab.edu*

Pic. 2-4 Retrieved from *indiabioscience.org*

References

Nizam Uddin and Thamina Acter. (2021). An Overview of Global Epidemics and the Challenges Faced. *PubMed Central*. Retrieved from https://www.ncbi.nlm.nih.gov/pmc/articles/PMC8342595/ on Oct. 20, 2023.

Interview with Dr. Findlay about Zoonotic Diseases. *ESL Lesson Plans*. Retrieved from https://www.linguahouse.com/en-GB/esl-lesson-plans/medical-english/infections on Oct. 20, 2023.

How Pandemics End. *BBC 6 Minute English*. Retrieved from https://www.bbc.co.uk/learningenglish/features/6-minute-english_2022/ep-220804 on Oct. 20, 2023.

Jillian McKoy. (2022). BU Researchers: We Have the Potential to Prevent Endemic Monkeypox. *Boston University*. Retrieved from https://www.bu.edu/articles/2022/bu-researchers-have-the-potential-to-prevent-endemic-monkeypox/? utm_campaign = bu_ today&utm_source=email_20220829&utm_medium=intrograph&utm_content=research_infectiousdiseases on Oct. 20, 2023.

Doug Most. (2022). How Worried Should We Be about Monkeypox? *The Brink*. Retrieved from https://www.bu.edu/articles/2022/how-worried-should-we-be-about-monkeypox/? utm_campaign=bu_today&utm_source=email_20220531&utm_medium=intrograph&utm_content=research_publichealth on Oct. 20, 2023.

Some People's Brain Function Still Affected by Long COVID Years After Infection. *King's College London*. Retrieved from https://www.sciencedaily.com/releases/2023/07/230721113224.htm on Oct. 20, 2023.

Major Epidemics of the Modern Era. *Council on Foreign Relations*. Retrieved from https://www.cfr.org/timeline/major-epidemics-modern-era on Oct. 20, 2023.

How to Prevent Infections. *Harvard Health Publishing*. Retrieved from https://www.health.harvard.edu/staying-healthy/how-to-prevent-infections on Oct. 20, 2023.

Interview with Dr. Ed Pertwee: Vaccine Hesitancy and Lessons Learnt. *European Science-Media Hub*. Retrieved from https://sciencemediahub.eu/2022/08/24/interview-with-dr-ed-pertwee-vaccine-hesitancy-and-lessons-learnt/ on Oct. 20, 2023.

One Health Is a Big Ask But It Can Save Us. *One Health Trust*. Retrieved from https://onehealthtrust.org/news-media/podcasts/one-health-is-a-big-ask-but-it-can-save-us/? gclid=EAIaIQobChMIiIjQgrLSgQMVyxF7Bx369QiREAAYAiAAEgIJafD_BwE on Oct. 20, 2023.

Cholera — Has Climate Change Given New Life to an Old Enemy? *One Health Trust*. Retrieved from https://onehealthtrust.org/news-media/podcasts/cholera-has-climate-change-given-new-life-to-an-old-enemy/ on Oct. 20, 2023.

The Video Message by United Nations High Commissioner for Human Rights at the Science and Technology in Society Forum Session "Shaping a Post-COVID Society". *United Nations*. Retrieved from https://www.ohchr.org/en/statements/2020/10/role-science-and-technology-post-covid-future on Oct. 20, 2023.

Getting a Good Night's Sleep Could Boost Your Response to Vaccination. *Cell Press*. Retrieved from https://www.sciencedaily.com/releases/2023/03/230313121003.htm on Oct. 20, 2023.

David Bass. (2023). What Is "Disease X" and Should We Be Worried? *Impakter*. Retrieved from https://impakter.com/what-is-disease-x-and-should-we-be-worried/ on

Oct. 20, 2023.

Simon Nicholas Williams. (2023). Vaccine Hesitancy Is One of the Greatest Threats to Global Health — and the Pandemic Has Made It Worse. *The Conversation*. Retrieved from https://theconversation.com/vaccine-hesitancy-is-one-of-the-greatest-threats-to-global-health-and-the-pandemic-has-made-it-worse-208227 on Oct. 20, 2023.

Unit 3 Employment

Part A Job Hunting

A1. Introduction

Job-hunting Strategies That Really Work

James Gonyea

Many job seekers view their job hunting as an unpleasant experience filled with frustration, stressful encounters with strangers, a loss of control over their life and an opportunity for personal failure. Job hunting can be difficult, but it doesn't have to be! With proper preparation and a good attitude, looking for the right job can be an opportunity to truly enhance your career.

Prepare for success

Finding a job requires preparation. To do it right, start with a thorough self-assessment that includes exploration of your work and school history, career goals, volunteer activities, hobbies, ambitions, values and needs. From this review, determine which occupations best match your personality style and then establish appropriate job-hunting goals.

Accentuate the positive

Just as important as good preparation is the right mental attitude. Job hunting will most likely take time, so pace yourself accordingly and be patient. It will also require you to occasionally operate outside of your comfort zone. Control your fear of the unknown, welcome the challenges that await you and be willing to explore new experiences. See the job search process as what it really is — an opportunity to explore and evaluate new career options that can add value and enjoyment to your life. Don't allow your fears to govern your behavior. It's difficult to see the real world when your head is buried in the sand.

Find the right strategy

Once you know what type of employment you're looking for, you're ready to start seeking a position. Use these strategies below to help you stand out to potential employers and land the job you want.

Use all job search resources

Use job search engines to find openings on job boards, company websites, professional associations and more. Sign up for daily or weekly job alerts by email. Rather than limiting yourself to manual online searches, take advantage of all job search options. This might include reaching out to companies or hiring managers in person, attending career fairs, searching social media or using a career counseling service.

Network regularly

Interact with people and develop professional contacts both online and in person. Start conversations with people at seminars, social events or appointments. Let them know you're looking for a job or want to work in a certain industry. They might have connections or advice that can help you in your job search. You might also discover unlisted job openings or people might recommend you for future opportunities.

Internships

If you are inexperienced, starting with an internship is a great way to build your résumé and create professional connections. With some internships, you may have the opportunity to transition into a full-time role. If this is the case, make sure to put in your best effort through the course of your internship.

Customize your résumé

Tailor your résumé to each job you are applying for. Study the job description to determine why you are a great fit. Then, add your skills, experience and measurable achievements that are relevant to that position. To simplify this step, have templates of your résumé and cover letter ready to customize.

Identify examples of your skills

People tend to remember engaging stories and examples over lists of facts. Plan ahead by identifying personal experiences or accomplishments that highlight the skills needed for a certain job. Add these to your cover letter and use them during networking opportunities or job interviews. Use the STAR method — situation, task, action, and result — to tell your story effectively.

Prepare for interviews

Review common interview questions, create responses for them and practice those responses before you get invited to an interview. Ask a friend or professional contact to do a mock interview with you.

Follow up

Immediately after a job interview, send the hiring manager a thank-you note. If you have not heard back from them after a week, follow up with a phone call or an email. When doing so, show your excitement and interest in the job. While you wait for a response, continue searching and applying for jobs that interest you.

(Adapted from *monster.com*)

A2. Words and Expressions

Vocabulary

1. advert /ˈædvɜːt/ *n.* 广告
2. well-versed /ˌwelˈvɜːst/ *adj.* 精通的，熟知的
3. align /əˈlaɪn/ *v.* 对准，使成直线
4. résumé /ˈrezəmeɪ/ *n.* 简历，履历
5. cover letter /ˈkʌvəˌletə/ *n.* 封面信，说明信，附函，求职信(常伴随其他文件一起出现并放在最上面，其作用是介绍其他文件的用处和目的)

Prep Work	**准备工作/求职**
search job adverts	搜索招聘广告

attend a job fair	参加招聘会
job opening	职位空缺
job seeker / job hunter / job applicant / job candidate	求职者
recruiting / hiring manager	招聘经理
fill out an application	填写申请表
fill a job vacancy	填补空缺职位
apply for an entry-level job	申请入门级工作
schedule an interview	安排面试
reject the interview invitation	拒绝面试邀请
perform research on the company	对公司进行调查研究
examine the job description	研究岗位描述
well-versed about the position	熟知职位情况
align with career goals	跟职业目标一致
a good fit for the role	该岗位的合适人选
keep the résumé up to date	更新简历
cover letter / covering letter	封面信,求职信
reference letter / recommendation letter	推荐信

Vocabulary

1. janitor /ˈdʒænətə/ *n*. 看门人,管理员(负责看护、打扫和维修,多见于办公楼、学校和公寓)
2. barista /bəˈriːstə/ *n*. 咖啡厅服务员
3. bartender /ˈbɑːrˌtendə/ *n*. 酒吧服务员
4. mixologist /ˌmɪkˈsɒlədʒɪst/ *n*. 调酒师
5. chambermaid /ˈtʃeɪmbəmeɪd/ *n*. (酒店内)打扫客房的女服务员
6. aerospace /ˈeroʊspeɪs/ *adj*. 航天航空的

Career Options	**职业选择**
plumber	管道工
janitor / caretaker	看门人
welder	焊工

electrician	电工
porter	搬运工，行李员
barista	咖啡厅服务员
bartender	酒吧服务员
mixologist	调酒师
chambermaid	打扫客房的女服务员
deliveryman	送货人，快递员
craftsperson	工匠，手艺人
undertaker	殡仪员
receptionist	接待员
interpreter	口译者
columnist	专栏作家
freelancer	自由职业者
pharmacist	药剂师
office clerk	办公室职员
junior accountant	初级会计
administrative assistant	行政助理
health care provider	医护人员
sales representative	销售代表
legal professional	法律从业人士
flight attendant	空乘人员
insurance agent	保险代理人
real estate broker	房地产经纪人
financial adviser	财务顾问
news anchor	新闻主播
online retailer	网络零售商
fashion photographer	时尚摄影师
film and TV producer	影视制作人
social worker	社会工作者
professional athlete	职业运动员
mental health counsellor	心理健康咨询师
scientific researcher	科学研究者
aerospace engineer	航天航空工程师
IT worker	信息技术工作者
call center agent	呼叫中心工作者（通过电话应答为客户提供信息或服务）
help desk technician	客服技术员（通过电话、电邮或网络向客户提供技术帮助）

Vocabulary

1. magna cum laude /ˌmæɡnəˈkʊmˈlaʊdeɪ/ *adv.* 以优异成绩地（拉丁语）
2. Ph.D. /ˌpiːeɪtʃˈdiː/ *n.* 博士，博士学位，哲学博士学位（全称 Doctor of Philosophy）
3. gap year /ˈɡæpˌjɪə/ *n.* 空档年，间隔年，休学年（中学毕业后上大学前所休的一年假期，通常用于旅游或打工）

Education and Work History	**教育与工作经历**
diploma	毕业文凭，学位证书
certificate	证书，证明
dissertation	专题论文，学位论文
academic degree	学术学位
be awarded with a scholarship	被授予奖学金
major in	主修
minor in	辅修
Bachelor of Arts (BA)	文学学士
Master of Science (MSc)	理学硕士
do a Ph.D.	攻读博士学位
graduate magna cum laude	以优异成绩毕业
comprehensive education	综合教育
vocational education	职业教育
compulsory course	必修课
optional course	选修课
refresher course	进修课程
pursue further education abroad	出国深造
gap year	空档年
relevant work experience	相关工作经历
work in public sector	在公共部门工作
work in private sector	在私营部门工作
volunteer experience	志愿者经历

internship experience	实习经历
on-job training	在职培训
get a promotion	获得晋升
career shift	职业变动
job hopping	跳槽
future prospect	未来前景
advancement opportunity	发展机会
benefits package	福利待遇
leave previous employer	离开前任雇主

Vocabulary

1. troubleshooting /ˈtrʌbəlˌʃuːtɪŋ/ *n.* 处理难题,调节,检修
2. meticulous /məˈtɪkjələs/ *adj.* 严谨的,注重细节的,一丝不苟的
3. integrity /ɪnˈtegrəti/ *n.* 正直,诚实

Skills and Personality	**技能与个性**
multi-task	同时处理多个任务
troubleshooting	处理难题
critical thinking	思辨思维
fast learning	快速学习
time management	时间管理
interpersonal skills	人际交往能力
hard skills and soft skills	硬技能和软技能
communication and negotiation skills	沟通和谈判技能
computational and data-processing skill	计算和数据处理技能
proficient in MS Office	熟练掌握微软办公软件
foreign language proficiency	外语水平
perform well under great pressure	重压下表现良好
make informed decisions	做出明智的决定
work in fast-paced environment	在快节奏的环境中工作
work with good initiative	积极主动地工作
self-motivated	自我激励的,积极主动的

analytical	善于分析的
apprehensive	有理解力的
meticulous	严谨的
a man of integrity	正直之人
good stress tolerance	抗压能力强

A3. Situational Conversations

Conversation 1 Attending a Career Fair

S: Sally C: Career Counselor

As a freshman, Sally is talking with a career counselor at her university.

S: Hi, Madam. Do you have a minute?

C: Sure. How can I help you?

S: I have a couple of questions about the **career fair** next week.

C: OK, **shoot.**

S: Um, are seniors the only ones who can go? I mean, they're finishing school this year and getting their degrees and everything... and, well, it seems like businesses would want to talk to them and not first-year students like me.

C: No, no. The career fair is open to all our students and we encourage anyone who's interested to go **check it out.**

S: That's good to know.

C: You've seen the flyers and the posters around campus, I assume.

S: Sure! Can't miss them. I mean, they all say where and when the fair is, just not who should attend.

C: Actually, they do. But it's in the small print. We should probably make that part easier to read, shouldn't we? I'll make a note of that right now. So, do you have any other questions?

S: Yes, um, since I'd only be going to familiarize myself with the process — you know, "check it out" — I was wondering if there's anything you'd recommend that I do to prepare.

C: That's a very good question. As you know, the career fair is generally an opportunity for local businesses to recruit new employees and for soon-to-be graduates to have interviews with several companies they might be interested in. Now, in your case, even though you wouldn't be looking for employment right now, it still wouldn't hurt for you to prepare much like you were looking for a job.

S: You mean like get my résumé together and wear a suit?

C: **That's a given.** I was thinking more **along the lines of** doing some research. The flyers and posters list all the businesses that are sending representatives to the career fair. Um, what's your major, or do you have one yet?

S: Well, I haven't declared a major yet but I'm strongly considering accounting. See, that's part of the reason I want to go to the fair... to help me decide if that's what I really want to study.

C: That's very wise. Well, I suggest that you get on the computer and learn more about the accounting companies, in particular, that will be attending. You can learn a lot about companies from their websites. Then prepare a list of questions.

S: Questions? So in a way I'll be interviewing them?

C: That's one way of looking at it. Think about it for a second. What do you want to know about working for an accounting firm?

S: Well, there's the job duties, probation, starting salary, and working conditions. And maybe about opportunities for advancement.

C: See? Those are all important things to know. After you do some research, you'll be able to **tailor** your questions to the particular company you're talking to.

S: Wow, I'm glad I **came by** here! It looks like I've got some work to do.

C: And if you plan on attending future career fairs, I recommend you sign up for one of our interview workshops.

S: I'll do that. Thanks for your information.

(Adapted from *top.zhan.com*)

☞**Notes**

- **career fair**: also known as job fair, an event where a large number of recruiters and potential employers gather for the purpose of providing information about available positions and their companies in general.
- **shoot**: used to tell someone that they should speak.
- **check it out**: to go to a place to see what it is like.
- **"That's a given."**: uttered when someone says something that is obviously true.
- **along the lines of**: similar in type.
- **tailor**: to make something so that it is exactly right for someone's particular needs or for a particular purpose.
- **came by (somewhere)**: to visit a place for a short time, often when you are going somewhere else.

Conversation 2 Talking about Career Planning

T: Ted J: Joe

T: Hi, Joe! You are graduating from university in a couple of months. Do you have any plans for the future?

J: It seems I have two options, either going to graduate school or hunting for a job. These are **bugging** me now.

T: Do you have a clear career path to follow?

J: Career path? I'm not sure.

T: What kind of job do you want after graduation?

J: I want to be a lawyer, a reporter or an editor.

T: Wait! What exactly do you want to do?

J: I have no idea at all. Any suggestions?

T: Yeah. You should first decide what kind of career you are really into, plan your career path, and then try your best to achieve your goal.

J: There're hundreds of career options out there. How can I decide which occupation is appropriate for me? I think perhaps I need to **buy a few years** while I figure out about my career.

T: No, Joe, you can't waste your time wandering around. Well, before you can make a career choice, I think you have to learn about yourself, to assess yourself. Why not use self-assessment tools or career tests online? Or you may simply ask a career development professional for help.

J: I understand. Could you be more specific about self-assessment?

T: Evaluate your strengths, preferences, work style and financial needs. Consider your work, education, and volunteer experiences. What have you enjoyed? What makes you **despondent**? If the idea of wearing a suit every day drives you nuts, you may not want to pursue a career in finance.

J: And then, what's the next step?

T: Then look over the list of occupations generated through self-assessment and come up with a shorter list for you to explore.

J: So I can cut down those jobs that I find unappealing?

T: Absolutely. After that, you need to research about the job description, requirements, job outlook, advancement opportunities, benefits **and all that jazz.**

J: Where can I get all that information?

T: You can search online, or ask friends who have the firsthand knowledge. If possible, interview people involved in your area of interest for information about their work, ask about the realities of the field and the recommended preparation for it. Also, internships and part-time jobs are an excellent way to **pin down** a field of interest.

They provide the opportunity to perform some of the job functions and evaluate the workplace environment.

J: Sounds great! What you suggested here is useful indeed, but I'm still a student.

T: You can consider applying for on-campus roles related to potential job interests. **Say**, if you're thinking about a journalism career, you might work for a campus magazine or newspaper. On the other hand, selecting project-oriented courses related to career options can also help you decide what's right for you. For instance, if you're considering product management as a career, you might select a marketing course where you **formulate** a branding campaign for a product.

J: There's a lot to do!

T: Surely there is. You will have to put some time.

J: Thank you so much, Ted. I really appreciate your suggestions.

(Adapted from *thebalancecareers.com*)

☞**Notes**

- **bug**: to annoy or worry someone.
- **buy a few years**: to buy time is to do something in order to be allowed more time.
- **despondent**: unhappy and with no hope or enthusiasm.
- **and all that jazz**: and other similar things.
- **pin down**: to find out (something) with certainty.
- **say**: used to attract attention to what you are about to say.
- **formulate**: to develop something such as a plan or a set of rules, and decide all the details of how it will be done.

Conversation 3 Job Hunting of a College Dropout

K: **Kelly** **N**: **Nicky**

K: How is your job hunting going, Nicky?

N: I haven't found a job yet, but I have a few **leads**, so things are **looking up**.

K: But isn't that what you always say?

N: Uh, this time is different.

K: What are you looking for this time, then?

N: Actually, I want to work for a web hosting company.

K: What would you do there?

N: Well, in a nutshell, web hosting companies provide space for people to store and run their websites. Does it sound like I know what I'm talking about?

K: Oh, yeah, **sort of**. And then?

N: They allow people to run their web sites without having to buy and maintain their own servers, and I'd like to work in technical support, you know, helping customers resolve computer-related problems with their sites. And you know I'm a good communicator.

K: So, how's the pay for that kind of job?

N: Well, most people I know start out with a very reasonable salary. You can earn pay increases depending on your performance.

K: What about benefits?

N: Oh, the benefits are pretty good. They provide health insurance, two weeks of paid vacation a year, and opportunities for advancement. And in the end, I'd like to work in a management position. You know, sitting back, enjoying the view out of the twentieth-story window of the office building. Something like that.

K: Okay, is there any long-term job security in a job like that?

N: Uh, that's hard to tell. I mean, the Internet is booming, and these kinds of companies are **sprouting up** everywhere, which is a good thing, but just like the dot-com era, you never know how long things will last.

K: That's true. Have you ever thought about going back to school to improve your job skills?

N: What are you suggesting, Kelly?

K: Well, frankly speaking, more training might help you land a better job.

N: Are you trying to say something about my current job at McDonald's?

K: You know, you did drop out of college.

N: I know. I'm just seeing my current job as a step up. Yeah, but I don't have the resources to go back to school at the moment. However, the job I am looking at will pay for some classes after I have been with the company for six months.

K: Well, it looks like you have things planned out this time.

N: If I last that long.

(Adapted from *esl-lab.com*)

☞ **Notes**

- **lead**: a piece of information that allows a discovery to be made or a solution to be found.
- **look up**: to get better or be improved.
- **sort of**: used to say that something is partly true but doesn't describe the exact situation.
- **sprout up**: If a large number of things sprout up, they suddenly appear or begin to exist.

Conversation 4 Preparing Credentials for Job Hunting

T: Tracy J: Jenny

J: Hey, Tracy, I saw this ad in the paper. It looks perfect for you.

T: What's it?

J: It's for a job.

T: Let me see. "Wanted: full-time English teacher for **up-and-coming** language school. Good professional and organizational skills. Experience a plus. Please contact Betty Sue." Oh, I don't know...

J: Come on, what have you got to lose?

T: I'm just unprepared! I haven't the faintest idea of how to go about finding a job!

J: Take it easy. Let's **dive right in** and see where to start.

T: I guess I should create a résumé first.

J: Sure. Making a good first impression is the key to landing any job, and that starts with your résumé.

T: Then I'll have to write it well.

J: Exactly. Make sure it's highlighting your strengths and experience that are most relevant to the position, as well as the value you'd bring to the company.

T: You mean here I should showcase my special skills and talents to impress the boss?

J: **You said it.** List your education and achievements by date. Begin with the most recent and move backward.

T: I see. Is that all there is to it?

J: No, you'd better attach one or two **references** to your résumé.

T: That's easy. My dean said he would give me a **glowing** reference.

J: Great! You also need to craft a cover letter to send with your résumé. Make it impressive enough to **knock their socks off!**

T: Wait, wait. What is a cover letter? Is it different from a résumé?

J: A résumé is an objective overview of your qualifications while a cover letter is a professional document used to introduce yourself to an employer. The purpose of a cover letter is to give you space to prove that your qualifications make you the best fit for a job opening. It's an opportunity to demonstrate more of your personality than you can on your résumé.

T: Wow, you really know the ropes. By the way, what's the format like?

J: A cover letter is structured in full paragraphs instead of bullet points, just like a formal letter.

T: OK. What about the length?

J: Aim for 250 to 400 words. Three or four paragraphs will suffice.

T: Reasonable. Recruiters don't have much time to read through pages.

J: Absolutely. Do tailor both your résumé and cover letter to the specific position, and **succinctly** hit your selling points. This may take a few rounds to perfect, but it'll be worth it.

T: That sounds a little stressful. How to send my materials, by the way?

J: Mostly, via mail or email. Find the name of a specific person at the company who you can address your materials to. This will ensure that the stuff ends up on their desk or in their inbox rather than floating around the office.

T: Good point!

J: In case of an email, you'd better send credentials as PDF attachments. There're many different word processors and not all are compatible with each format. Proofread everything you've written beforehand!

T: I know, it has to be typo-free. Do I need to follow up with a phone call or email?

J: Surely, after about a week if you haven't heard anything. Good luck.

T: Thank you so much, Jenny. You're a real help. I'll come back to you soon.

J: Anytime.

(Adapted from *indeed.com*)

☞**Notes**

- **up-and-coming**: likely to achieve success soon or in the near future.
- **dive right in**: to start doing something suddenly and energetically, often without stopping to think.
- **"You said it."**: used to say that you agree with what has just been said.
- **reference**: a letter written by someone who knows you, to describe you and say if you are suitable for a job, course, etc.
- **glowing**: praising with enthusiasm.
- **knock their socks off**: If something knocks your socks off, you find it extremely exciting or good.
- **succinctly**: something succinct is said in a clear and short way without unnecessary words.

A4. Picture Knowledge

Vacancy

Admin and HR Executive

We are a fast growing food company with a central bakery and four upscale sales outlets. Our business is to provide our customers with food that is delicious, food that is nutritious and nourishing and to create a work place that is rewarding to all of its stakeholders. We have a vacancy for an Admin and HR Executive who can do a multitude of management tasks as outlined below.

Responsibilities

- Maintain employee files, assist with payroll, keep track of confirmation dates, coordinate appraisals, maintain leave records and implement HR activities to improve effectiveness and efficiency.
- Handle maintenance issues of the company and the outlets.
- Handle purchasing of packaging materials and stationery.
- Assist the marketing team by scheduling of advertisements, coordinate events and assist with new product launches.
- Secretarial work for MD — maintaining company files, handle correspondence of the company.

Experience and Qualities Required

- A degree or professional qualification preferably in human resource management.
- Excellent written and verbal English skills.
- A sound knowledge of employment and labour law.
- Minimum 2 years HR and / or administration experience.
- Proficiency in MS Office (Word / Excel / Outlook).
- Good administrative, documentation and communication skills.
- Able to work independently and with good initiative.
- Meticulous and able to multi-task.

Please send in your CV with details of two non-related referees within 7 days of this advertisement to ***hr@lpf.lk*** or by post to:

Lanka Premier Foods Pvt. Ltd
84, Lorenz Road, Colombo 04.
***Phone**:011 4 388 488*

Attractive salaries and the opportunity to move up in a growing food service company awaits the right candidate.

Pic. 3-1 Job vacancy

Cover Letter

OPENING

To Whom It May Concern, / Dear Sir or Madam,

REASON FOR WRITING

I am writing to express my interest in the position of...
I wish to apply for the position of...
I am writing in response to your advertisement for...
I am writing to enquire as to whether there are any vacancies...

INTRODUCING YOURSELF

I am currently working as... / I am currently studying...
At present, I am working for... where I am responsible for...
I have been working in my current position for the past (time).

TALIKING ABOUT YOUR EDUCATION & EXPERIENCE

I graduated from ABC University with a degree / master's degree in...
The nature of my studies has prepared me well for a position such as this one.
As you can see from my CV, I have worked... and gained experience...
My mother tongue is English and I am fluent in both French and German.

WHY YOU ARE THE BEST FOR THIS POSITION

I feel I am suitable for this role as I have a great deal of experience in...
I consider myself to be a friendly, efficient and enthusiastic worker.
I believe I would be the ideal candidate based on the fact that I...
I am very keen to work for an ambitious company such as yours.

CLOSING COMMENTS

Thank you for taking time to consider my application.
I am available for contact and / or interview at any time.
If you wish to contact me, you can do so on +353 898889...
Should you require further information, do not hesitate to contact me.
Please find CV attached (emails) / enclosed (letters).

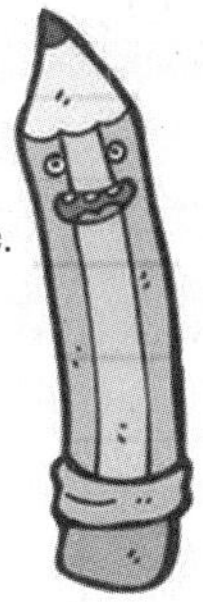

SIGNING OFF

I look forward to hearing from you.
Your sincerely, (If you know the name "Dear Mr. John")
Your faithfully, (If you are writing to "Dear Sir or Madam")

Pic. 3-2 Cover letter format

Entry-level Cover Letter

your.name@gmail.com (123) 456-7890 142 Your Address Blvd, City Name, CA 12345

Hiring Manager's Name
341 Company Address
Palo Alto, California 94301
(555) 239-5678
hiring.manager@gmail.com

Dear [Hiring Manager's Name],

As a long-term admirer of the impressive work being done by the team at Mayflower Technologies, I'm delighted to submit my application for the entry-level IT technician opening posted on LinkedIn. As a recent graduate from the University of Rochester with a B.S. in Computer Science, I'm confident that my knowledge of Linux systems, experience in backend coding, and precise attention to detail would make me an asset to the team at Mayflower.

In my former role as a student worker at the University of Rochester's Technical Services department, I was responsible for troubleshooting a variety of technical issues for staff, assisting with server maintenance, and installing a wide range of equipment. While employed there, I assisted in the development and rollout of new department practices, and helped improve our ticket response time by 12%. I'm sure that this experience will help me start contributing quickly at Mayflower.

I also understand that Mayflower is seeking to expand their cloud computing services. While at the University of Rochester, I specialized in and completed my thesis on cloud computing. The IT technician position at Mayflower is an exciting opportunity for me to use this educational background, as well as learn more about a growing industry.

I've attached my résumé, which further details my skills and education. Please do not hesitate to reach out if you have any questions, and I look forward to the opportunity to speak with you further. Thank you for your time and consideration.

Sincerely,

[Your Name]

Pic. 3-3 Entry-level cover letter

RECENT GRADUATE RÉSUMÉ SAMPLE

Robin.James@gmail.com
895 555 555
4397 Aaron Smith Drive Harrisburg, PA
linkedin.com/in/r.james

SKILLS
Problem Solving
Adaptability
Collaboration
Time Management
Critical Thinking
Interpersonal Skills
Leadership

LANGUAGES
Native: English
Fluent: Spanish
Proficient: Farsi

AWARDS
Dean's List
NYU / Last 3 Semesters
Tau Sigma Honors Society
NYU / 2019

RÉSUMÉ OBJECTIVE

Recent college graduate with a degree in Political Science. Designed and led a statewide polling project in New York to gauge public opinion on tort reform. Seeking to leverage 3.8 GPA and data analysis expertise to obtain the political research assistant position at Win Blue.

EDUCATION

Bachelor of Arts in Political Science / GPA: 3.8
New York University , New York City , Graduated 2020
Relevant Coursework: International Politics, Economics, Public Polling, Data Analysis, Electoral Process
Honors: magna cum laude

RELEVANT EXPERIENCE

THE ELECTION PROCESS AND PUBLIC OPINION
Senior Seminar, NYU / October 2019 — May 2020
- Developed a thesis proposal for a statewide public opinion poll on tort reform.
- Awarded a $1,000 grant to expand and execute my polling research.
- Formulated a series of 10 questions designed to reduce bias.
- Polled over 1,000 New York residents, reaching the threshold for statistical significance.
- Organized the resulting data and presented my findings to the NYU Political Science department.

VOLUNTEER
Tom Suozzi for Congress. New York, May 2018—November 2018
- Made and distributed campaign materials to supporters.
- Helped lead get out the vote efforts in local neighborhoods, knocking on over 800 doors.
- Wrote scripts for other campaign volunteers to follow when phone banking.
- Excelled in a fast-paced, demanding environment.

Pic. 3-4 Recent graduate résumé sample

Professional Reference Email Sample

Subject line: Derrick White — Reference

Dear Ms. Chin,

I'm writing to recommend Derrick White. I've worked with Derrick for the past five years at ABC Event Planning Company; for three of those years, he was my direct report.

In the time I've known him, Derrick has consistently been a strong employee — capable of taking control of big projects and executing to the fullest. As well, he's a pleasure to work with. Derrick is cheerful in the face of daunting deadlines and always available to lend a hand to co-workers when necessary.

Rarely do you come across someone who is talented at both big picture ideas and executing the small details — Derrick is just that person. As an account supervisor here at ABC Event Planning Company, he pitches event plans to clients and then manages the client relationship from ideation through execution. Derrick would be a great fit for your company, building strong relationships and ensuring successful events.

I highly recommend Derrick as an employee at your company. He would be an asset to any organization. Please do not hesitate to be in touch if you have any further questions.

Best,

Tanisha Jones

Director, ABC Event Planning Company
jonestan@email.com

555-555-5555

Pic. 3-5 Professional reference email sample

CV

Thomas Henderson | Physics Graduate

Location:**Luton**
Telephone:**07777777777**
Email:**Thomas@ThomasHenderson.com**

Professional Profile

"A skilled Physics Graduate with a proven academic and practical understanding of geophysics, quantum physics and atomic physics"

With significant experience in the oil and gas industry I am skilled in testing and researching seismic data and can use advanced and sophisticated geo equipment and devices. I have hands-on experience in both planning and conducting experiments, alongside trend analysis and the development of new theories. I also have expertise in the use of a variety of physiological research software systems, specifically Fortran 90.

Core Skills

- Practical and academic physics experience
- Data analysis
- Trend analysis
- Technical reporting
- Computational and data-processing skills
- Planning and conducting experiments
- Theory development
- Knowledge of mathematical modelling

Education & Qualifications

- **BSc (hons) Physics, 2:1** — Luton University—2020
  Dissertation: Quantum Effects in Biology
  Modules studied include: Classical mechanics, Introduction to quantum physics, Mathematical methods for physics, Experimental physics and computing, Quantum and atomic physics
- **4×A Levels, grades A*AAB** — Luton College—2016
  Physics, Chemistry, Maths, Further Maths
- **12×GCSEs, grades A*-B** — Luton School—2014
  Achieved A*-B in subjects including: Maths, Physics, Chemistry, IT, English Literature and Language

Physics Experience

June 2018—June 2019 XYZ Fuel Inc, London
Outline **Geophysics Intern (University Placement)**

Working for a UK based oil and gas company, assisting the established team to study what lies below the earth's surface to create effective mining maps.

Key Responsibilities

- Assisted the Geophysicists to plan projects prior to attending site visits
- Designed data acquisition plans
- Agreed on suitable seismic measurement and data-processing techniques for each project
- Monitored the reactions of recording equipment to detect irregularities
- Accurately interpreted and mapped 2D and 3D seismic data
- Drafted reports discussing collected seismic data which were then finalised by the Lead Geophysicist and issued out to the wider team, clients, senior managers and partners
- Measured reservoir volumes
- Assessed potential oil and gas yields
- Supported the team to design, test, modify and repair seismic equipment
- Reviewed and made suggestions to amend and improve data collection procedures
- Generated charts to display the results of a variety of testing procedures
- Complied documentation and ensured work logs remained up to date

Key Achievement / Projects

- Successfully identified the location of an oil reservoir and 3 potential drilling locations which were later pursued by the company.
- Identified two process improvements which reduced project costs by an average of 7%.

Page 1

Pic. 3-6 CV

Continued

June 2017—Sept 2017 ABC Research Co, London
Physics Intern

Outline

Summer Internship working at a UK leading research company, responsible for supporting research projects relating to the evaluation of new hardware or software technology and the development of a functional prototype instrument.

Key Responsibilities

- Supported the Research and Development Team to develop and evaluate new technology including assisting in the design, modelling, analysis, testing and troubleshooting processes
- Tested prototype products in the laboratory, supporting the Lead Researcher to characterise and optimise instrument performance
- Worked closely with product experts and potential customers to thoroughly understand their requirements and specifications
- Ensured project tasks were completed within the agreed timescales

Key Achievement / Projects

- Maintained a 100% error-free data record during the period of the internship.

Career Summary

June 2016 — Present **Fashion4U, Luton**

Outline **Sales Assistant (Part Time)**

Working for a large fashion retailer with 28 stores across the UK. Reporting to the Store Manager, being responsible for providing exceptional customer service, processing orders, and maintaining the store.

Key Responsibilities

- Offered customers a warm welcome
- Assisted customers with any queries including making product suggestions, locating items, and providing information about in store offers and promotions
- Processed cash and card transactions using a POS system
- Ensured the store stock was maintained and the store remained clean and tidy

Key Achievement / Projects

- Regularly exceeded sales targets by over 20% through providing exceptional customer service and appropriate product recommendations.
- Achieved the maximum mystery shopper result of 100% on 2 separate occasions.
- Developed and implemented a new stock management system which increased the efficiency of the process by over 30%.

Additional Information

Professional Memberships Student member of the institute of Physics

IT Skills MS Excel, MS Access, Fortran 90, AIP4WIN, MATLAB

References Available on Request

Page 2

Pic. 3-6 CV

A5. Follow-up Activities

Brainstorm

What are the similarities and differences between a CV and a résumé? Could you list the situations when you are supposed to submit a CV instead of a résumé?

Writing

Perform some research and learn to create your own résumé. Here is a simple guide to the basics of writing a good résumé.

- Write your full name and contact details at the top of the résumé.
- Include an objective description of the work you hope to obtain.
- Summarize your education and work experience.
- List your qualifications and skills.
- Finish your résumé with "References Available upon Request".

Pay attention to the following tips:

- Be concise and short. Your finished résumé should not be more than a page.
- Use dynamic action verbs such as accomplished, collaborated, facilitated, etc.
- Use tenses in the past. Except for your present job.

(Adapted from *thoughtco.com*)

Presentation

Please give a presentation on the topic — **my dream job.**

You may mention the following aspects:

- your dream job when you were a kid.
- your dream job when you grow up.
- qualifications and skills needed for the job.
- the most challenging part about the job.
- reasons why you love the job.

You may refer to the expressions below but don't confine yourself to them.

Suggested Expressions:

decide on my career choice
shape my career in a better manner
decent and high-paying job
engaging and rewarding job
entry-level job
advance into management
self-motivated and well-informed
stay positive about difficulties
reach out to people
job satisfaction
job security
remuneration package

take a leadership position
make life-enriching products
make a mark in the industry
work nine to five
work flextime
work overtime
a mix of technical and soft skills
esprit de corps
committed and accountable
passionate and creative
advancement opportunity
short commute
work life balance
corporate culture
work alongside great talents
make myself stand out
a good fit for the job
dream it possible
The hours aren't punishing.
The pay feels fair.

Interpretation

Interpret the following paragraphs into English with what you have learned in Part A.

Paragraph 1

大四下学期我开始准备求职的相关材料。首先，创建个人简历。我将学术背景、相关经历、所获荣誉、资格证书等信息按照时间顺序呈现出来，并认真设计简历的布局和样式。其次，准备推荐信。我请系主任和一位曾教过我两年专业课的教授分别为我写推荐信，我敢保证，他们的推荐信一定会助我一臂之力。最后，撰写封面信。我参考网上的模板，认真研究如何将个人背景和特长与将要申请的职位准确对接，并用简洁有力的语言向未来雇主推销自己。

Paragraph 2

我在校园里看到了一场招聘会的海报和宣传页，虽然我正在读大三，尚未进入求职阶段，但还是决定去现场一探究竟，提前了解一下招聘流程和就业前景。我是学市场营销的，重点关注了与专业相关的空缺职位。有一家总部在广州的房地产公司很是吸引我，他们的招聘职位是具有销售或营销专业背景的实习生或兼职人员，有工作经验者优先。我立即就岗位职责、申请条件、薪资待遇等诸如此类的问题咨询了招聘经理并记下了对方的联系方式。

A6. Extension

Synonym Discrimination

Can you figure out the differences among the words below?

Group 1: diploma / degree / certificate / certification
Group 2: job / career / occupation / profession / vocation / trade
Group 3: despondent / depressed / dispirited / dejected

Extensive Reading

Important Personal Skills That Employers Value

Alison Doyle

Candidates with strong personal skills are in high demand for a wide variety of jobs. We've all worked with someone who is excellent at engaging with colleagues and is always dependable. These individuals have honed their personal skills. They communicate effectively with others, self-express, and self-manage.

Your personal skills shape not only your professional trajectory, but your private life as well. Overall, employers look for job candidates with strong personal skills because they positively contribute to the office culture, and are reliable in a variety of ways.

What are personal skills?

Unlike hard skills that can be measured, like computer programming skills or legal knowledge, personal skills are soft skills — intangible qualities or traits that enhance our interactions. They are just as, if not more, important to employers, though you'll need a mix of both.

Strong personal skills are critical to your success in any job, as they allow you to work well with employers, employees, colleagues, clients, and vendors.

Those with strong personal skills can communicate ideas clearly and listen well to others. They also exude a positive attitude at work, which is key to any healthy company culture.

Company leaders seek employees with personal skills because they are better able to effect positive outcomes for their companies. These individuals are typically more reliable, meet deadlines, and complete tasks. In addition, these subjects are motivated and passionate about their work, which contributes to their success.

Types of personal skills

Below is a list of the most important personal skills that most employers look for. It also includes sublists of related skills that employers tend to seek in job applicants. Develop and emphasize them in job applications, résumés, cover letters, and interviews.

Critical thinking

Employers want candidates who can solve problems on their own using creative thinking and make informed decisions using thoughtful analysis. Critical thinkers are useful in every industry, from healthcare and engineering to education. Whether you are a restaurant manager, an engineer, or a teacher, you need to be able to understand problems, think critically, and devise solutions. Skills required for critical thinking include creativity, problem-solving, and curiosity.

- Creativity
- Critical observation
- Critical thinking
- Curiosity
- Flexibility
- Innovation
- Logical thinking
- Research
- Resourcefulness
- Thinking outside the box
- Tolerance of change and uncertainty
- Troubleshooting
- Value education
- Willingness to learn

Problem solving

How well do you solve problems? Problem-solving is going to come up in virtually every job. Employers value strong problem solvers, as they effectively and swiftly make decisions while largely keeping their emotions at bay. They gather as much information as they can and let intuition, logic, and innovative thinking drive the best solution. Being a great collaborator and open to the ideas and opinions of others is also very important. So be sure to highlight your ability to work with others to find the best solution.

- Accuracy
- Assertive
- Conflict management
- Decision making
- Diplomatic
- Humble
- Influential
- Intuitive
- Patience
- Perceptive
- Practical
- Reflective
- Teamwork
- Insightful

Flexible & dependable

Dependability and flexibility work in tandem, as flexible employees are always dependable, and vice versa. Employers hire candidates who demonstrate reliability, responsibility, and trustworthiness. Flexible employees can adapt to change, take on projects outside of their scope, and shift their schedule if necessary. A flexible and dependable employee is also willing to help their colleagues with projects, even when the subject matter is unfamiliar.

- Accountable
- Adaptability
- Competence
- Honesty
- Loyal
- Punctual

- Dynamic
- Helpfulness
- Teachable
- Reliable
- Responsible
- Trustworthy

Interpersonal skills

Interpersonal skills, also known as people skills, are those related to how you communicate and interact with those around you. Employers want employees who are compatible with their employers, their colleagues, and clients. It is a particularly important trait when collaboration is encouraged, and those who embody it will climb the ladder more quickly than their counterparts.

Being a good listener is key to being a strong communicator. Employers want employees who can both share their own ideas and also listen empathetically to others. Listening is a very important skill in customer service, human resources, and in all leadership positions.

Displaying such skills will impress your potential employer and could lead to future opportunities for promotions and raises.

- Articulate
- Attentiveness
- Collaborative
- Conscientiousness
- Considerate
- Empathy
- Inclusive
- Listening
- Negotiation
- Nonverbal communication
- Professional
- Relationship building
- Respectful
- Sense of humor
- Sincere
- Sociable
- Storytelling
- Understanding
- Verbal communication
- Persuasion

Intrinsically motivated

Employers seek employees who are positive and passionate about their jobs and are motivated by internal forces. These individuals tend to put the most effort into their work and learn from their mistakes and failures. These individuals also tend to enjoy the process far more than those motivated by money and glory, thus making these candidates more pleasant to work with and trustworthy in the eyes of employers.

- Ambition
- Alertness
- Confidence
- Dedication
- Determination
- Independent
- Optimism
- Positive
- Resilience
- Strong work ethic

- Energy
- Hardworking
- Visionary
- Productive
- Enterprising
- Passion

More personal skills

Below are additional personal skills for résumés, cover letters, job applications, and interviews. Required skills will vary based on the job for which you're applying.

- Compassionate
- Effective communicator
- Ethical
- Function well under pressure
- Generosity
- Self-awareness
- High emotional intelligence
- Team player
- Integrity
- Trainable
- Meet deadlines
- Willing to accept feedback
- Performance management
- Positive work ethic
- Process improvement
- Quick-witted
- Results-oriented
- Self-supervising
- Stress management
- Time management
- Tolerant
- Knowledge management
- Memory skills
- Personal development

(Adapted from *thebalancecareers.com*)

Part B Job Interview

B1. Introduction

Useful Phrases for Job Interviews in English

Abigail Lister

So, you've written a fantastic cover letter and been invited to a job interview — great job! Now it's time to prepare for that all-important conversation. Any job interview is always going to be nerve-wracking, but even more so if you're doing the interview in your second language.

Anyone will tell you that being prepared is the most important key to success in these situations, and that covers not only dressing well and knowing the role inside and out but also making an impression with your language. We've compiled the most important phrases to keep in mind as you try to impress your interviewer, from the moment you step through the door to following up afterwards. With these phrases, you'll be one step closer to securing your dream job!

How to start the interview

There's no better time to start making an impression than the moment you step through the door. Make an effort to be polite and exude confidence when you meet your interviewer — without coming across as arrogant.

- I'm pleased to meet you!
- Thank you for taking the time to meet with me today.
- I really appreciate being considered for this role.
- I'm looking forward to talking about my skills and experience.

Describing your skills

Make sure to highlight your skills in every question you get asked, and don't be afraid of talking too much about a skill you think is relevant for the role. Explain your educational background and highlight any additional qualifications that might set you apart from other candidates — including any language test scores.

- I graduated from... in... with a degree in...
- I am qualified in...

- I completed a course in... which gave me skills in...
- I have an IELTS certificate with a score of...

Explaining your experience

When you talk about your past work experience, it's important to focus on your achievements, rather than just explaining what you were responsible for or what you did day-to-day. If you can, include real data about what you achieved, whether this is how many sales you made or how much money you saved the company.

- In my role at... I succeeded in...
- I am proud of the work I did at...
- An example of a problem that I solved is...
- I consider my strengths to be... and I think these are important for this role because...
- I have a proven track record in...

Answering questions about your future

If you get asked about your plans for the future, try to link achievable, though perhaps distant, plans with the role that you are applying for. This will make you look even more motivated, and show the interviewer that you'll work hard in the position.

- In five years' time, I'd like to be responsible for... and I believe this role is the first step to achieving that.
- This role aligns with my long-term career goals, which are...
- I would like to build my career at this company because...

Asking questions to your interviewer

As the interview comes to a close, this is your chance to take control and ask anything you'd like to know of the position or the company. Make sure to have at least a few questions prepared, as not only will it demonstrate your enthusiasm, but you'll get to see if the job is a good fit for you as well. If you don't have any questions, you could finish by explaining again how you fit the role, and ask about the next steps.

- I was doing some research on the company and I found out... I really admire this, can you explain more about it?
- Can you tell me about the long-term goals for this company?
- Are there any training programs available to employees?
- What do you enjoy most about working here?
- I just want to reiterate again that I think my experience and background really fit

this role because...

- Could you explain what the next steps are?

Phrases for after the interview

Even after the interview is over, there's still time to make a good impression! Make sure to follow up with a thank-you note in an email either the same day or the day after the interview, where you could also outline your skills again and why you think you fit the role.

(Adapted from *esl-languages.com*)

B2. Words and Expressions

Vocabulary

1. panel /ˈpænəl/ *n*. 专门小组
2. credential /krɪˈdenʃəl/ *n*. 资历,资格,资格证书
3. jitter /ˈdʒɪtəz/ *n*. (事前的)紧张不安(常用作复数)

Before the Interview	**面试前**
in-person interview	当面面试
panel interview	小组面试
video interview	视频面试
phone interview	电话面试
screening interview	筛选面试
search the location in advance	事先寻找(面试)地点
conduct a mock interview	进行模拟面试
do a test run	演练,试运行
brush up interview skills	复习面试技巧
practice sample interview questions	练习面试样题
review your questions to ask	回顾你要提问的问题
refine and commit answers to memory	提炼并记住答案
practice out loud	大声练习
practice body language	练习肢体语言

print hard copies of credentials	打印资历资格证书
prepare appropriate attire	准备合适的服装
prepare a checklist of items to bring along	准备一份随身携带物品清单
get the jitters	紧张不安

Vocabulary

1. assertive /əˈsɜːtɪv/ *adj*. 坚定自信的，果敢的
2. off-color /ˌɑːfˈkʌlə/ *adj*. (言论或笑话)粗俗的
3. monopolize /məˈnɑːpəlaɪz/ *v*. 独占，霸占，垄断
4. fiddle /ˈfɪdəl/ *v*. 无目的地拨弄或摆弄
5. slouch /slaʊtʃ/ *v*. 没精打采地站、坐或走
6. ramble /ˈræmbəl/ *v*. 语无伦次地说
7. babble /ˈbæbəl/ *v*. 含糊不清地说

During the Interview	**面试中**
follow the etiquette	遵守面试礼仪
show up on time	准时出现
arrive way too early	太早到达
dress the part / act the part / look the part	穿着得体 / 行为得体 / 看起来得体
well-groomed	穿着整洁的
wear light and natural makeup	化自然的淡妆
sit up straight	坐得笔直
stay focused and attentive	集中注意力
rid oneself of distractions	摆脱干扰
come across as assertive	表现得坚定自信
put one's best foot forward	展现自己最好的一面
give a professional impression	给人一种专业的印象
make an opening statement	做开场陈述
get the interviewer on one's side	使面试官支持自己
tie one's qualifications to the job	将某人的资历与工作关联
set one apart from others	使自己与众不同

excel at	擅长
showcase the strength	展示优点
state the weakness	陈述弱点
highlight relevant skills	突出相关技能
address the question directly	直接回答问题
give a thoughtful answer	做出深思熟虑的回答
gather the thoughts before responding	回应之前认真思考
frame the answers around positive aspects	围绕积极因素来构建答案
ask industry-specific questions	问某行业特有的问题
ask open-ended questions	问开放式的问题
ask for clarification	要求澄清、解释
avoid off-color humor	避免粗俗的幽默
make preventable errors	犯可避免的错误
show up late on short notice	临时告知迟到
monopolize the conversation	独占谈话
go into too much detail	过于详细
moan about a former employer	抱怨前雇主
sell oneself	推销自己
sell oneself short	贬低自己
fiddle	摆弄东西
slouch	无精打采
ramble	语无伦次
babble	含糊不清

Vocabulary

1. poised /pɔɪzd/ *adj*. 做好准备的，摆好姿势的
2. shortlist /ˈʃɔːrtlɪst/ *n*. 最终候选名单
3. tank /tæŋk/ *v*. 彻底失败，输掉

After the Interview	**面试后**
the most nerve-wracking part	最伤脑筋的部分

evaluate the performance	评估表现
inform the references	通知推荐人
stay poised for future opportunities	为未来的机会做好准备
stand a better chance of success	成功的机会更大
put someone on the top of the shortlist	将某人放在最终候选名单首位
follow up with the employer	跟进雇主的情况
give a follow-up call	事后打个电话
drop a thank-you letter	写封感谢信
put in a good word for someone	为某人说好话
hear back from the company	公司有答复
get into the next round	进入下一轮
grow one's personal network	扩大个人关系网
continue the job search	继续找工作
screw up / mess up an interview	搞砸面试
bomb / tank an interview	面试失败
nail ace an interview	面试成功
land a job	得到一份工作

B3. Situational Conversations

Conversation 1　A Job Interview (with a Fresh Graduate)

C: Cindy　G: Ms. Gordon

As the HR manager, Ms. Gordon is interviewing Cindy who has just graduated from university.

G: Nice to meet you, Cindy. I'm Monica Gordon from the Department of Human Resources. Please take your seat.

C: Nice to meet you, Ms. Gordon.

G: Your **CV** is very impressive. You have done well in your academics and have got through **with flying colors**! You did B.E. in computer engineering and proceeded to do MBA and specialized in strategic management instead of doing Master under the same graduation subject. Is there any particular reason for it?

C: Um, I felt that a technical degree along with Master in management would help me move upwards in my career.

G: Exactly! That's why you are here for this interview. We are looking for fresher with such an educational combination to take on as trainees. Why do you think you are the right candidate for this job?

C: Well, I'm always interested in news about your industry, and I'm deeply impressed by your company's sales performance. It is an incredible **feat** to have risen 200% in the domestic market over just the past three years. I also admire the values that the company has adopted. I find that my personal goals and ideas about business operations fit perfectly with the company's mission statement.

G: So you are well aware of our company. It appears that you have done your fair share of research.

C: Yes, I believe that it's also crucial for me to know if the company is right for me. I've been impressed by the service provided here by everyone from the receptionist to the assistant. I'm confident that I'll have a very rewarding career here.

G: Thanks for your compliment. Commitment to the team and the company is very important to us here.

C: Yes, I know. I'm cooperative and responsible. I enjoy **intermingling** and working with others. My teacher and classmates could always count on me to work out functional solutions.

G: So what are your career objectives? And how do you perceive your own development if you were to **assume** this position?

C: I'm awaiting a good opportunity to put all of my knowledge into practice. I'm a **go-getter** and I could become a contributor to the company very quickly. Honestly, I hope I could lead a productive team within five years.

G: Good, then do you have any questions about our company or the position?

C: Yes, may I know how long the training will be?

G: The training will take six months. Initially, it will be held in our headquarter. Later, the trainees will be shifted to the regional offices for **on-the-job** training for another six months.

C: I see. Is there any exam to be passed at the end of the training?

G: No exam as such. But you will be assessed for your performance through the entire training period.

C: All right. When can I expect to hear from you?

G: We'll get back to you early next week. You see, we have scheduled a number of interviews for this week. You have a bright chance, Cindy. Best of luck!

C: It was nice meeting you. Thanks for your time.

(Adapted from *learningenglishessentials.com*)

☞ **Notes**

- **CV**: abbreviation for curriculum vitae, a short written description of your education, qualifications, previous jobs and sometimes also your personal interests, that you send to an employer when you are trying to get a job.
- **with flying colors**: If you do something with flying colors, you do it very successfully.
- **feat**: something difficult needing a lot of skill, strength, courage, etc. to achieve it.
- **intermingle**: to become mixed together.
- **assume**: to take or begin to have responsibility or control.
- **go-getter**: someone who is very energetic, determined to be successful, and able to deal with new or difficult situations easily.
- **on-the-job**: happening while you are at work.

Conversation 2　A Job Interview (with a Job Hopper)

P: Mr. Parsons　R: Rebecca　S: Sally (secretary)

P: Come in.

R: Mr. Parsons?

P: Ah, you must be Rebecca. Please do come in.

R: Thank you for making some time to see me, Mr. Parsons. It's a pleasure to meet you finally.

P: The pleasure is all mine. Have a seat, please. Now would you like any refreshments? Tea or coffee?

R: A coffee would be lovely. Thank you.

P: No problem. Sally, can we have two coffees please? One black, no sugar.

S: Certainly, Mr. Parsons.

P: So Rebecca, you had a first interview with Ms. Childs last week.

R: Yes, she **filled me in** on the details of the job on the telephone.

P: Great. I'm glad to say she recommended you for a second interview, and here we are. Rebecca, I think you've given us a clear idea of your positive qualities, but can you share a weakness?

R: Certainly. I do tend to get frustrated if I don't see progress in my work or career. I suppose I'm quite a restless character. My father always taught me to be a high achiever.

P: So would you say if things don't go your way at work, it could easily get you down?

R: In a way, yes. But I must say that even if I'm not completely happy in my work, I always give 110%. I would never **shirk** my responsibilities. I guess sometimes I expect too much too soon.

P: You know, journalism is a highly competitive world, so you do need to keep pushing yourself. Okay, let's move on to your work experience, shall we?

R: Yes, please.

P: After graduating from university, your first job was...

R: I started with a local newspaper as an intern. I was really keen on getting some experience in the journalistic world, and this seemed like a good first step.

P: Certainly. And after your internship?

R: They offered me a position as a junior news reporter. I was in charge of the sports news section. I really enjoyed it there, and it helped me build my skills.

P: And then you left and spent almost four years at the *City Weekly*, is that right?

R: Yes. The first year was quite tough for me. Well, slowly but surely, I proved myself, so the editor promoted me to a **feature** writer.

P: Wow, a real step up! But you decided to leave them in 2020, why?

R: It was a hard decision to make. I enjoyed my time at my last job, but I felt like I was in a comfort zone and I needed to **shake things up** in my life. I was ready for a more challenging role.

P: That makes sense. Rebecca, I think we've covered all the main points. Here's my business card. If any other questions **spring to mind**, please feel free to contact me or Ms. Childs. We'll be in touch.

R: Thank you so much for the interview, Mr. Parsons. I'm looking forward to hearing back.

P: Absolutely. Thanks for coming. Bye.

(Adapted from *kekenet.com*)

☞ **Notes**

- **fill me in:** to give me extra or missing information.
- **shirk:** to avoid work, duties or responsibilities, especially if they are difficult or unpleasant.
- **feature:** a special article in a newspaper or magazine, or a part of a television or radio broadcast, that deals with a particular subject.
- **shake things up:** to make a big change in the way something is organized.
- **spring to mind:** to come quickly into your mind.

Conversation 3 Getting the Job Offer

I: Interviewer S: Sarah

I: Hello, Sarah, thanks for coming today.

S: You're welcome.

I: Now, why don't you start by telling me about your employment background.

S: Sure. I have been a marketing professional for the last ten years. I studied marketing at university and have worked in various marketing roles.

I: What are some of the industries you've worked in?

S: I have worked in telecommunications, financial services, travel agency and recruiting.

I: What would you say your strengths are?

S: My strengths are in creating systems and processes to get the job done quickly and manage **contractors** and staff efficiently. This helps save time and money for my employers.

I: What would you say your weaknesses are?

S: My weakness is using statistical software such as **SASS**. I find it difficult to navigate.

I: Why do you think you would be a good addition to this team?

S: I am a very industrious worker, and I am a team player. I believe in producing high-quality work and focusing on getting the job done. I have the technical skills and the experience required to work well with your team and deliver results.

I: Why did you leave your last job?

S: I decided to leave my last job because I wanted the opportunity to grow and excel with a high performing team, and I felt that I have gone as far as I could with my previous employer.

I: Where do you want to be in three years?

S: I want to be working for your company in a leadership role.

I: Do you have any questions about the job?

S: Yes, I do. Why has this job become available?

I: This job role opened due to a demand in the business to respond to the changing nature of online marketing. We need a specialist to help us better **leverage** our digital assets.

S: What would you say are some challenges this role would **encompass**?

I: I would have to say that there are many levels of management, and you will need to be able to navigate through all of the stakeholders to ensure that you can get the job done with the right approvals.

S: I see. What is the vision for the company for the next two years?

I: The company is in an aggressive growth phase. The focus is to increase market share by 20%.

S: That's very interesting. Those are all of the questions that I have.

I: Well, that's all for the interview. Thank you, Sarah. I think you get the job offer. Congratulations!

S: Thank you so much! I'm so ecstatic! It's a big honor for me to join you.

I: Welcome aboard! What other questions do you have, Sarah?

S: Could you tell me a little about the working hours?

I: Um, our working hours are not exactly nine to five. You could be on call at any time. We do have to work very unsocial hours at times.

S: I'm used to that, so that's not really a shock for me.

I: Good, as long as you understand that.

S: When would you like me to fill the vacancy, Sir?

I: How about starting from the beginning of next month?

S: That sounds perfect.

(Adapted from *english-for-students.com*)

☞**Notes**

- **contractor**: a person or company that arranges to supply materials or workers for building or for moving goods.
- **SASS**: abbreviation for Syntactically Awesome Style Sheets.
- **leverage**: to use something that you already have in order to achieve something new or better.
- **encompass**: to include.

B4. Picture Knowledge

Thank-you Email After Interview

To Recipient

Recipient's email

Subject

Re:

Cc:

Dear (Ms. J. Doe),

I would like to thank you very so much for your time during our interview on (Monday 29th, last week). I was both nervous and excited by the opportunity and it was an absolute pleasure to meet you. You managed to make me feel welcome and at ease within the first 5 minutes which allowed me to be truly myself.

The position of (name of position), its responsibilities and challenges are exactly what I have been searching and hoping to find in a job. Being a part of (name of company) would prove to be both challenging and rewarding to me; two magic ingredients that I believe are required so as to compliment the person undertaking the tasks at hand.

I feel that I am the perfect candidate for this opening due to my past experiences, industry knowledge and passion for what I do.

I look forward to your decision and should you require any further information or references from my current or past employers, please just let me know and I will be happy to be able to provide you with what you need.

I may be reached on: (insert tel. Number).

Looking forward to hearing from you.

Kind regards,
(signed name)

Pic. 3-7 Thank-you email after interview

Rejection Letter

Subject Line: [Title of Position] — Job Application

Dear Ms / Mr Name,

Thank you for taking the time to meet with me for the [Job Title] role at [Company Name].

It was a pleasure to meet you and learn more about your skills and accomplishments. I have now had the opportunity to consider all the candidates and regret to inform you that on this occasion we have decided to not further your application.

This decision has been tough as the overall standard of the candidates has been high. However, we found that during the test, the other candidate had higher numerical skills. We would advise gaining further experience in the field and reapplying in the near future when more positions become available.

Thank you again for your interest in [Company Name]. I wish you every success in your job search and career.

Regards,

Name

Job Title

Company Signature

Pic. 3-8 Job application rejection letter

Job Offer Rejection Letter

August 30, 2020
Simon Jones
1737 Marshville Road, Alabama
United States

To,
Ted Smith
Personnel Director
Vital Aids Ltd.
35, Amphitheatre Parkway
Mountain View, CA 94043
United States

Dear Mr. Smith,

I'd like to thank you for offering me the position of Media Consultant in your organization. After much consideration, I have reached the conclusion that I shall accept the offer from another company where at this point in my career the position I have been offered aligns more closely with my interests, potential, and continued success.

I sincerely appreciate that you took out your valuable time to take my interview and offer me this role. It was a pleasure meeting you and your team. I would like to stay in touch with you at LinkedIn to share social media practices.

Kind Regards,
Dave Mason

Pic. 3-9 Job offer rejection letter

B5. Follow-up Activities

Brainstorm

Make a list of things that you should do before and after an interview. When finished, share your list with the class.

Individual Work

Review these most frequently asked interview questions, and then prepare your responses based on your own experience, skills, and interests. Remember that it's less about providing the "right" answers and more about demonstrating that you're the best candidate for the job.

1. Tell me about yourself.
2. Why are you interested in this position?

3. What is your greatest strength?
4. Could you share a weakness?
5. Why did you leave your previous job?
6. What are your career goals?

(Adapted from *thebalancecareers.com*)

You may refer to the expressions below but don't confine yourself to them.

Suggested Expressions:

I see myself as a top-performing person who ______.
This position fits perfectly with my ______.
My background as a ______ major will help me to ______.
My ______ years of experience in ______ enables me to ______.
I pride myself on my ______ skills.
What makes me unique is my ability to ______.
One area I improved on in the past is ______.
I valued my time at my previous company, but it's time to ______.
In five years, I'd like to ______.
Some of my future goals involve ______.

Role Play

You and your partner will take turns interviewing each other. First, decide who will be the job seeker and who will be the interviewer. Next, choose one of the given job openings to apply for. Then, work in pairs and role play a mock interview.

Student A (job seeker): Suppose that you have the appropriate background for the position. Bring your résumé and other documents you may need, and prepare your answers to common interview questions.

Student B (interviewer): Decide how to structure the interview and what questions to ask. You may cover the questions listed in Individual Work. List the qualifications and traits that a qualified job candidate should possess. Finally, you may make a decision about the interviewee.

Position: Sales Intern at a Fortune 500 company
Location: Shanghai, China
Duties:
— researching and generating lists of potential customers
— providing input on customer briefs, presentations and sales literature
Skills:
— basic sales techniques
— good interpersonal and communication skills
— proficient in PowerPoint, Excel, Word & EndNote
Requirements:
— major in Sales, Advertising or Marketing
— 3.0 GPA or higher
Benefits:
— gaining hands-on experience
— collaborating with experienced sales professionals
— compensation available

(Adapted from *internships.com*)

Position: Research Assistant at a pharmaceutical company
Location: Hong Kong, China
Duties:
— maintaining a safe and organized lab bench
— purchasing and preparing chemicals, reagents and samples
— retrieving necessary scientific information from online resources
Skills:
— exceptional research skills
— PubMed, Google Scholar & Scopus
— proficiency in written and spoken English & Mandarin
Requirements:
— MS or above in Biochemistry or Chemical Engineering
— basic knowledge of scientific principles
— ability to work in a fast-paced team environment

(Adapted from *jobs.com*)

Interpretation

Interpret the following paragraphs into English with what you have learned in Part B.

Paragraph 1

我刚刚大学毕业，拥有经济学学士和法律硕士学位，目前正在找工作。我在网上看到一家外企的招聘广告，招聘职位是法律顾问，我对此很感兴趣，并且认为自己是一个合适的人选。首先，该职位和我的学术背景高度匹配，我可以学以致用；其次，我很认同该企业的文化和发展理念，愿意在此开启我的职业生涯。于是，我填写了网上申请表并附上更新过的个人简历，期待着面试邀请。

Paragraph 2

在经历了电话筛选面试之后，我成功进入了下一轮的现场面试。在面试当天，我提前半个小时来到指定地点，仔细查看了打印的简历、相关学历证书和模拟面试时做的笔记。我提醒自己在面试官面前要表现得专注和专业，充分展示我的优势和个性，同时避免答非所问、含糊其辞。事实证明，我的确做到了！由于面试非常成功，人力资源部经理当场决定录用我并于次日对我进行在岗培训。

B6. Extension

Synonym Discrimination

Can you figure out the differences among the words below?
Group 1: skill / craft / art / technique
Group 2: fire / quit / sack / dismiss / resign

Extensive Reading

Strengths and Weaknesses for Job Interviews

Ed Moss

There are certain questions that recruiters love to ask their candidates, and two of the most popular ones are undoubtedly:

- "What's your greatest strength?"
- "What's your greatest weakness?"

Many job seekers get stuck in these interview questions. Yes, it can be hard to identify your own strengths and weaknesses. If you've never known how to answer them — keep reading as we go through ten strengths and ten weaknesses that will make you look like the ideal applicant during your interview!

Good answers for "What's your greatest strength?"

Flexibility

Example: "I'm able to handle change. In my previous job, I worked with several different clients and had to be flexible enough to jump from one project to the other without jeopardizing my performance, which has taught me a lot about versatility." This also means that you are adaptable, versatile, and adjustable.

Dedication

Example: "I'm extremely passionate about what I do and that shows in my work. When I'm involved in a project, I give my 110% and make the results we're achieving for the client are as fruitful as possible. I use my dedication and eagerness to accomplish goals efficiently and effectively." This also means that you are passionate, effective, and loyal.

Positive attitude

Example: "My biggest strength is my positive attitude. I know how stressful this industry can get, but I'm able to keep my calm and power through by focusing on the end goal and I've been told in the past that this attitude has had a positive impact on my colleagues." This also means that you are upbeat, motivated and forward-thinking.

Creativity

Example: "I love being creative and developing solutions that are completely out-of-the-box. In my previous job, I had the opportunity to work on a tech project that was all about innovation and creativity, and we ended up receiving three industry awards for our results." This also means that you are a problem solver, innovative, and clever.

Leadership skills

Example: "I've been a natural leader ever since I can remember and for the past 15 years, I've had the opportunity to use these skills in my career, managing a large digital marketing team. In my previous job, I was promoted to team leader after one year of working there and ended up working closely with the agency's CEO." This also means that you are a captain, able to guide and lead.

Determination

Example: "I've never been one to give up, even on my personal life, and that personality trait has definitely transpired into my career. When I'm involved in a project, I like to feel like I actually contributed to it in a significant way and that's what feeds my determination and focus." This also means that you are motivated, focused, and decisive.

A particular hard skill

Example: "My writing skills are very strong: I've been a copywriter and content creator for the past ten years and during this decade, I've had the chance to learn from some of the best in the industry. So much so, that my work has been published in *Forbes*, *Entrepreneur*, and other major publications."

Organization skills

Example: "After being in the labor market for six years, I know I can never perform to the full of my abilities when things are messy, whether it is my desk, my laptop, or my brain. Knowing this has allowed me to work on my organizational skills, and to develop working processes that help me ensure I never miss a deadline." This also means that you are efficient, process-oriented, and a systems thinker.

Empathy

Example: "Relating to people and understanding their emotions and needs is something that has always come naturally to me, and that might even explain why I've started my career in customer service. In my previous job, I got a call from a customer who was not satisfied with our service, and I was able to defuse the situation, explain what had happened and how we could make it up to him." This also means that you are caring, thoughtful, and a listener.

Continuous learning

Example: "I've been working in finance for two years now and one of the most important things for me has been continuous learning and improvement. I know I have so much in my career to look forward to and I want to be as prepared as possible, which is why I've been investing in relevant online courses for the past year." This also means that you are curious, wise, and seek knowledge.

Good answers for "What's your greatest weakness?"

The secret to answering this question is to find a weakness that won't damage your chances of being hired, but that proves to the recruiter that you're self-aware. Even the CEO of the company has their weaknesses, so this question is nothing to be afraid of! Remember not only to mention the weakness but also explain how you're working on it. This will show that you take initiative for yourself and are invested in your continuous learning!

Impatience

Example: "I've been told before that I can be quite impatient and I am aware of the fact that, when involved in a project, I can sometimes be a bit too eager to finish them. I'm working on that by learning how to prioritize my tasks and respect others' priorities as well." This also means that you can be eager and unmindful.

Self-criticism

Example: "During the past year, I've become too critical of myself, always focusing on what more I could have done, instead of what I achieved. I could tell that this was starting to have an impact on my well-being, so I decided to get help from a professional coach and I can confidently say that it has made a huge difference in my mindset." This also means that you can be too introspective.

Too direct

Example: "I've been told by coworkers that I can sometimes be too blunt with my feedback. That doesn't come from a place of malice, I've always been extremely straightforward, but I've realized that not everyone knows that. I decided to take a communication skills course and am now able to convey my feedback a lot better." This also means that you can be straightforward, and blunt.

Delegation skills

Example: "Sometimes I have a hard time delegating tasks because I want to be in control of the entire project. I've learned over the years that this isn't possible and by speaking with other professionals that had the same issue, I've been working on my delegation skills." This also means that you can be controlling, protective and demanding.

Disorganized

Example: "I'm not always the most organized person and, although that hasn't had a major impact on my work, I know having a cluttered desk isn't ideal for me or for my surrounding coworkers. I've been striving to organize my desk at the end of each day, to make sure I come back to a clean, tidy workstation." This also means that you can be irrational and disjointed.

Public speaking

Example: "Public speaking makes me nervous and I know this is an area I can, and should, work on. Although it isn't an essential skill for this particular position, I know it's still important for me to speak up during meetings, which is why I've recently enrolled in a public speaking boot camp." This also means that you can be often looked-over.

Insecure

Example: "I've always been a shy person and that has led me to feel a little insecure about sharing my ideas, particularly in a group setting. I'm aware that this can prevent me from taking incredible opportunities, so I've started going to improve classes. This has helped me feel a lot more confident about speaking up." This also means that you can be restrained and quiet.

Too detail-oriented

Example: "Sometimes I focus so much on a certain detail that I lose sight of the whole project and that has caused me and my team leader to stress out for no reason in the past. I've learned from those situations and nowadays make a concerted effort not to get lost in the details." This also means that you can be micro-managing.

Very introverted or extroverted

Example: "Anyone who knows me knows how introverted / extroverted I am. This can be an advantage at times, but I'm aware it can also be a weakness. I've gotten feedback on this from previous coworkers and managers, and have been working to find a healthy balance between my personality and my job." This also means that you can be over-the-top (if extroverted) or below-the-radar (if introverted).

A Particular hard skill

Example: "I'm still not familiar with the most recent programming language, which although isn't essential at the moment, is something I want to work on, as I know it can benefit both of us in the future. I've been looking for online courses so I can start one as soon as possible."

(Adapted from *easyresume.io*)

Sources of Pictures

Pic. 3-1 Retrieved from *dreamjobs.com*
Pic. 3-2 Retrieved from *careerchoiceguide.com*
Pic. 3-3 Retrieved from *indeed.com*
Pic. 3-4 Retrieved from *résumégenius.com*
Pic. 3-5 Retrieved from *thebalancecareers.com*

Pic. 3-6 Retrieved from *standout-cv.com*
Pic. 3-7 Retrieved from *templatelab.com*
Pic. 3-8 Retrieved from *wordtemplatesonline.net*
Pic. 3-9 Retrieved from *qwikrésumé.com*

References

James Gonyea. (2021). Job Hunting Strategies That Really Work. *Monster*. Retrieved from https://www.monster.com/career-advice/article/job-hunting-strategies-that-really-work.

Attending a Career Fair. *Top.Zhan*. Retrieved from http://toefl.zhan.com/tpo65964.html on August 5, 2021.

Career Planning. *The Balance Careers*. Retrieved from https://www.thebalancecareers.com/career-paths-4161858 on August 5, 2021.

Job Hunting. *Randall's Esl Cyber Listening Lab*. Retrieved from https://www.esl-lab.com/difficult/job-hunting-script/on August 5, 2021.

Indeed Editorial Team. (2021). Résumés and Cover Letters. *Indeed Career Guide*. Retrieved from https://www.indeed.com/career-advice/résumés-cover-letters/ résumé-vs-cover-letter.

Kenneth Beare. (2019). Writing Your Résumé. *ThoughtCo*. Retrieved from https://www.thoughtco.com/writing-your- résumé-1210230.

Alison Doyle. (2020). Important Personal Skills That Employers Value. *The Balance Careers*. Retrieved from https://www. thebalancecareers. com/personal-skills-list-2063763.

Abigail Lister. (2021). Useful Phrases for Job Interviews in English. *ESL Stories*. Retrieved from https://blog.esl-languages.com/blog/career/useful-phrases-for-job-interviews-english.

A Job Interview. *Learning English Essentials*. Retrieved from https://learningenglishessentials.com/english-conversation-topics-a-job-interview/ on August 5, 2021.

A Job Interview. *Kekenet*. Retrieved from http://talk. kekenet. com/show _ 578 on August 5, 2021.

Dave Pearl. (2019). Getting the Job Offer. *English For Students*. Retrieved from http://www.english-for-students.com/Easy-English-Conversations-37.html.

Alison Doyle. (2021). Top 10 Job Interview Questions and Best Answers. *The Balance Careers*. Retrieved from https://www. thebalancecareers. com/top-interview-questions-and-best-answers-2061225.

Sales Intern Job Description. *Chegg Internships*. Retrieved from https://www.internships.com/employer/resources/internships/sales-intern-job-description on August 5, 2021.

Research Assistant. *Jobs*. Retrieved from https://www.jobs.com/en-us/jobs/q-research-assistant-jobs on August 5, 2021.

Ed Moss. (2021). Strengths and Weaknesses for Job Interviews. *Easy Résumé*. Retrieved from https://www.easyresume.io/career-advice/strengths-and-weaknesses-for-job-interviews.

Unit 4 Travel Tips

Part A Weather

A1. Introduction

How Does Weather Affect Our Life ?

This is a very important question. Weather has a tremendous effect on people's daily lives. For instance, it is raining today and looking outside I see far fewer joggers and bikers out today than on typical sunny days in Santa Barbara. People who are outside are wearing warmer (and more) clothing than they normally do, and are making no attempt to linger outside or sun bathe, but instead hurry around to try to rush back inside as fast as possible.

As long as we were on the topic of weather, we might as well discuss climate too. It is commonly said, climate is what you expect (or predict), and weather is what you get. This is another way of saying that weather represents the conditions at a specific location on a specific day, while climate is the average conditions over many years. Both have a great impact on how we live, but climate tends to affect lifestyle, social structure, and culture, whereas weather affects daily choices such as those described above. Weather and climate to a large degree determine how we stay warm (or cool) enough to survive, how (and if) we stay comfortable, what modes of transportation we use, what type of clothing we wear, what foods we can grow and eat in an area, and what resources (such as water and trees) are plentiful or rare.

Weather sometimes has some less obvious effects on the way we live, too. For instance, weather patterns control the ocean as well as the land. During storms, we see bigger waves that carry away more sand from our beaches and can destroy kelp forests, washing huge mats of drift kelp onto the beaches. If you are a scuba diver or surfer, these factors will have an important effect on your recreational life. Storms also cause a lot of run off to wash dirt from streets into rivers and streams and out to the ocean, where they may have an impact on bacteria levels in the ocean (many surfers supposedly get sick from bacteria in the water after large storms). Weather patterns can also control fish populations in some areas and have a large effect on fishermen that harvest these fish (and the people who eat the fish).

Here in southern California, it doesn't rain very often so most farmers have to irrigate their fields with water from elsewhere in order to grow food. This creates competition for limited water resources between farming and other interests, such as drinking water, recreation (e. g., swimming pools) and landscaping. Climate and weather strongly control what fruits and vegetables can grow. For instance, next time you visit the supermarket, look at the labels on the fruits and vegetables to see where they are from. Many of them will likely be from California because we can grow a huge variety of food here for two reasons: there are many different climates in California, and many of the climates are favorable for the growth of many of the foods we like to eat. However, you may find some foods that are not grown in California for one of two reasons: that fruit or vegetable cannot grow well enough here to be farmed (such as pineapples), or that fruit or vegetable only grows during certain seasons here and so must be imported from other countries when it is not growing here (such as grapes and apples).

Another important aspect of weather that has a huge effect on our lives is extreme weather events, such as hurricanes, droughts, fires (forest fires), floods, heat waves, or cold snaps and winter storms. For instance, about a dozen people died last year in La Conchita when an anomalously wet rain season caused landslides that buried several houses. The summer before last, thousands died in Europe during an extreme heat wave, and thousands died recently in the southeast during a horrible hurricane season. Some of these extreme events may be consequences of climate change caused by humans and the burning of fossil fuels, while others are just periodic events that happen very infrequently. In many cases, these extreme events are more catastrophic now due to higher human populations. For instance, droughts that cause crops to fail and water sources to dry up are probably harder on areas with many people to feed and water than on areas with fewer people.

There is really no end to the ways that weather and climate affect our lives. I encourage you to look at the things you do on a daily basis and think about how they are affected by the weather and climate. Also think about how you live might change when the weather changes here or if different extreme weather events were to occur in this area.

Finally, think about how weather changes that occur elsewhere might affect the way you live. For instance, if there were a drought in an area that grows foods that you eat, how would your shopping and eating habits be affected?

(Adapted from *ucsb.edu*)

A2. Words and Expressions

Vocabulary

1. azure /ˈæʒə/ *adj*. 天蓝色的，蔚蓝色的
2. scorching /ˈskɔːrtʃɪŋ/ *adj*. 灼热的，极热的
3. dapple /ˈdæpəl/ *n*. 斑点，斑驳

Sunny Weather	**晴天**
fine / fair / nice	（天气）晴好的
azure	天蓝色的
clear / bright	晴朗的
clear up	放晴
cloudless	无云的
shiny / sunny	阳光灿烂的
bluebird day	（下雪后）晴朗无云的天气
mild sun	温和的阳光
scorching sun	烈日
glaring sun	耀眼的太阳
a patch of sunlight	一缕阳光
dapples of sunshine	树下斑驳的阳光

Vocabulary

1. draught /dræft/ *n*. （令人不适的）对流风，穿堂风
2. monsoon /mɑːnˈsuːn/ *n*. 季风，雨季

Windy Weather	刮风天气
gentle / light wind	微风
moderate wind	中度风
strong wind	大风,强风
gust	阵风
squall	飑,突然发作的强风
howling wind	比较大的风
blast	一阵疾风
breeze	微风
draught	穿堂风
gale	暴风
high winds	疾风
gusty	刮风的,起风的
swirling	打旋儿的
upwind	逆风地
downwind	顺风地
headwind	逆风
favorable wind	顺风
northeaster / southeaster...	(较大的)东北风 / 东南风
a breath of air	一丝风
monsoon	季风
Wind picks up.	风变大。

Vocabulary

1. frigid /ˈfrɪdʒɪd/ *adj*. (天气或室内温度)寒冷的,严寒的
2. arctic /ˈɑːrktɪk/ *adj*. 极其寒冷的
3. nippy /ˈnɪpi/ *adj*. (天气或空气)寒冷的

Cold Weather	冷天
chilly	冷的
cool	凉快的
bleak	阴冷的

crisp	干冷的
bitter	严寒的
brisk	清冷的
bone-chilling / biting	刺骨的
freezing	极冷的
wintry	冬天的，寒冷的
frigid	寒冷的，寒带的
frosty	严寒的，霜冻的
nippy	寒冷的，刺骨的
arctic	北极的，极寒的
subzero	零下的
wrap up warm	穿暖和
bundle up	多穿衣服
I cannot handle / stand the cold.	我怕冷。

Vocabulary

1. sultry /ˈsʌltri/ *adj*. （天气）闷热的，湿热的
2. sweltering /ˈsweltəɪŋ/ *adj*. 热极了，热得难受的
3. torrid /ˈtɔːrɪd/ *adj*. 炎热的，灼热的

Hot Weather	**热天**
close	闷热的
dog days	很热的天，三伏天
stuffy	（室内）闷的，不通气的
muggy / sultry	闷热的
sweltering	热极了
torrid / tropical	炎热的
blistering hot	酷热的
oppressive	闷热的，令人窒息的
scorcher	大热天
thermometer breaker	大热天

Vocabulary

1. temperate /ˈtemprət/ *adj*. (气候)温带的，温和的
2. balmy /ˈbɑːmi/ *adj*. (气候)温和宜人的

Mild Weather	**温和的天气**
calm / still	风平浪静的，无风的
dry	干燥的
fair	天气很好的
mild	温和的
seasonable	天气合时宜的
temperate	温和的
warm	温暖的
balmy	宜人的

Vocabulary

1. murky /ˈmɜːki/ *adj*. 黑暗的，不清楚的
2. overcast /ˈoʊvəkæst/ *adj*. 阴天的，多云的，布满阴云的
3. leaden /ˈledn/ *adj*. 深灰色的，灰蒙蒙的

Cloudy Weather	**阴天**
cloudy	多云的
lowering	(天气、天空)阴沉沉的，昏暗的
murky	黑暗的，阴沉的
overcast	阴天的
shady / dull / dim	阴沉的
sunless	没有太阳的
dark	天色暗的
leaden	灰蒙蒙的
pitch dark	漆黑的

Vocabulary

1. drizzle /ˈdrɪzəl/ *n*. 细雨,零星小雨,毛毛雨
2. lashing /ˈlæʃɪŋ/ *adj*. 大雨猛降的

Rainy Weather	雨天
spit	零星小雨
drizzle	毛毛雨
sprinkle	零星小雨
shower	阵雨
thunder shower	雷阵雨
sun shower	太阳雨
constant rain	阴雨连绵
downpour	瓢泼大雨
lashing	大雨猛降的
cloudburst	暴雨
freezing rain	冻雨
soaking wet	湿透的
humid	(空气、天气)潮湿的
damp	潮湿的,潮乎乎的
moist	潮湿的,湿润的
soupy	潮湿难耐的

Vocabulary

1. flurry /ˈflɜːri/ *n*. 小阵雪
2. icicle /ˈaɪsɪkəl/ *n*. 冰柱,冰锥

Snowy Weather	雪天
frost	霜
light snow	小雪
moderate snow	中雪

heavy snow	大雪
sleet	雨夹雪
flurry	小阵雪
snow flakes	雪花
snow fall	下雪
snowdrift	雪堆
snowbank	雪堤，很深的积雪
slush	雪泥
snow shower	阵雪
hail	冰雹
black ice	(路面上结的)透明薄冰
icicle	(屋檐滴水形成的)冰柱
thaw	解冻
melt	融化

Foggy Weather	**有雾天气**
fog	雾
haze	雾霭，霾
mist	薄雾
smog	(污染产生的)烟雾
rise	起(雾)
lift / clear	(雾)散，放晴

Vocabulary

1. foul /faʊl/ *adj*. 极其令人不快的，恶劣的
2. inclement /ɪnˈklemənt/ *adj*. (天气)恶劣的(尤指寒冷、有暴风雨或暴风雪)
3. cyclone /ˈsaɪkloʊn/ *n*. 旋风，气旋
4. torrential /tɔːˈrenʃəl/ *adj*. (雨)倾泻似的，如注的
5. blizzard /ˈblɪzəd/ *n*. 暴风雪，雪暴

Bad Weather	**恶劣天气**
foul	天气恶劣的
inclement weather	恶劣天气
extreme weather	极端天气

changeable weather	变化无常的天气
unseasonable weather	反常的天气
heat wave	酷暑
heat dome	热穹顶
cyclone	旋风
hurricane	飓风
typhoon	台风
tornado	龙卷风
dust storm	沙尘暴
rain storm	暴雨
torrential rain	倾盆大雨
blizzard / snowstorm	暴雪
hailstorm	雹暴

A3. Situational Conversations

Conversation 1 Talking about the Weather at Lunchtime

J: Jane L: Lucy

J: Hi, do you want to go and get some lunch?

L: Yes, that would be great.

J: I want to try the new café on the corner of the **High Street**.

L: Are you sure? It's very small and we may have to sit outside.

J: Yes, that's why I want to go. It's autumn already and the weather might not be good for eating outside again until the spring.

L: It looks as if it might rain soon. There has been some drizzle this morning.

J: No, the sky is clear and you can see the sun. That will make it warm.

L: But there's a gusty wind that makes it a bit chilly.

J: We can wear our coats. It's been overcast for weeks. I want to sit in the sun for a bit.

L: OK, but if it starts to snow we have to go inside, alright.

(Adapted from *excellentesl 4u.com*)

☞**Notes**

- **High Street**: a street where the most important shops and businesses in a town are.

Conversation 2 First Time to See the Snow

T: Tui A: Andrew J: Jane

T: Hi, isn't the snow great? I've been playing in it all morning.

A: Yes, new snow makes everything look very pretty and white.

J: Snow is nice at the start, but when it's turning to slush, it gets nasty.

T: Maybe, but this is the first time I've ever seen snow. It's great.

J: Do you ever have snow in Thailand?

T: No, we never have snow. It's too hot.

A: So, this must be fun?

T: Yes, very fun. I stayed up late last night watching the snowstorm as the gusts of wind blew the snow.

J: Then this morning the sky was clear and the sun was shining on the new snow. That was good to see.

T: How long will the snow last before it melts?

A: If the weather and temperature stay cold at about zero **degree Celsius**, then the snow could be here for several days or a week.

T: Great. I want to play in it as much as possible. Do you want to come outside with me?

J: Sure, I can do that.

A: Yes, that'll be something good to do.

(Adapted from *excellentesl 4u.com*)

> ☞**Note**
>
> - **degree Celsius:** a unit of temperature on the Celsius scale, a temperature scale originally known as the centigrade scale.

Conversation 3 Talking about Natural Disasters

T: Todd I: Ivan

T: Hi, Ivan. I heard that you are from Houston.

I: Yeah, and you are from California? Are there any natural disasters there?

T: Yes, Ivan. Here in California, we have earthquakes. Sometimes in summer, the extreme dry weather can cause wildfire. What about Houston?

I: Uh, it floods a lot and we get hurricanes. Houston's called a **bayou** city. Bayou is kind of like a dirty river.

T: Why does the river flood?

I: Sometimes it rains a lot, that thing fills up over, and the next thing you know you got water in your house.

T: That's a bit annoying.

I: But hurricanes are even worse. The first hurricane I ever remember (we name our hurricanes, you give them names, usually girl names), and the first hurricane I remember was back in 1984 named "Hurricane Alice" I believe. Um, I was in a soccer camp. It started raining, and the trees were falling down and cars were kind of being pushed away and I was scared to death. I was only seven years old at that time.

T: Wow, you must feel desperate. Did you ask anyone for help?

I: I couldn't remember my parents' phone number and the camp counsellors were trying to look it up. My mom answered the phone and told me not to worry about it. It was just a rain storm. But it was an absolute mess. The next day, the soccer field was completely **wiped out**. It was, yeah, a big angry storm.

T: How long does a hurricane usually last?

I: Usually, about two or three days.

T: Oh, that's too bad.

I: Yeah, they just kind of stay in Houston. They like Houston. Something about the weather pattern. They just float to Houston and stay there.

T: Man, that's pretty intense. So afterward everything is just kind of wiped out.

I: Ah, a lot of windows are broken. Sometimes a lot of cars are upside down, because the wind is really, really high, plus you got the water that floats the cars, but it's fun when it stops because the streets are flooded and you can go swimming.

T: You swim in the water?

I: Sure. It's just rain water.

(Adapted from *elllo.org*)

☞**Notes**

- **bayou**: a creek, secondary watercourse, or minor river that is tributary to another body of water.
- **wipe out**: to eliminate something completely.

A4. Picture Knowledge

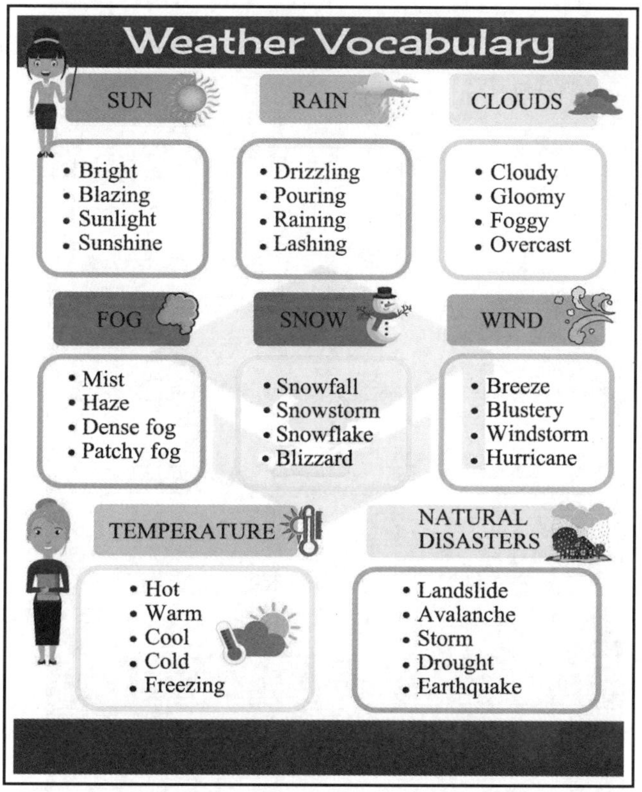

Pic. 4-1 Weather vocabulary

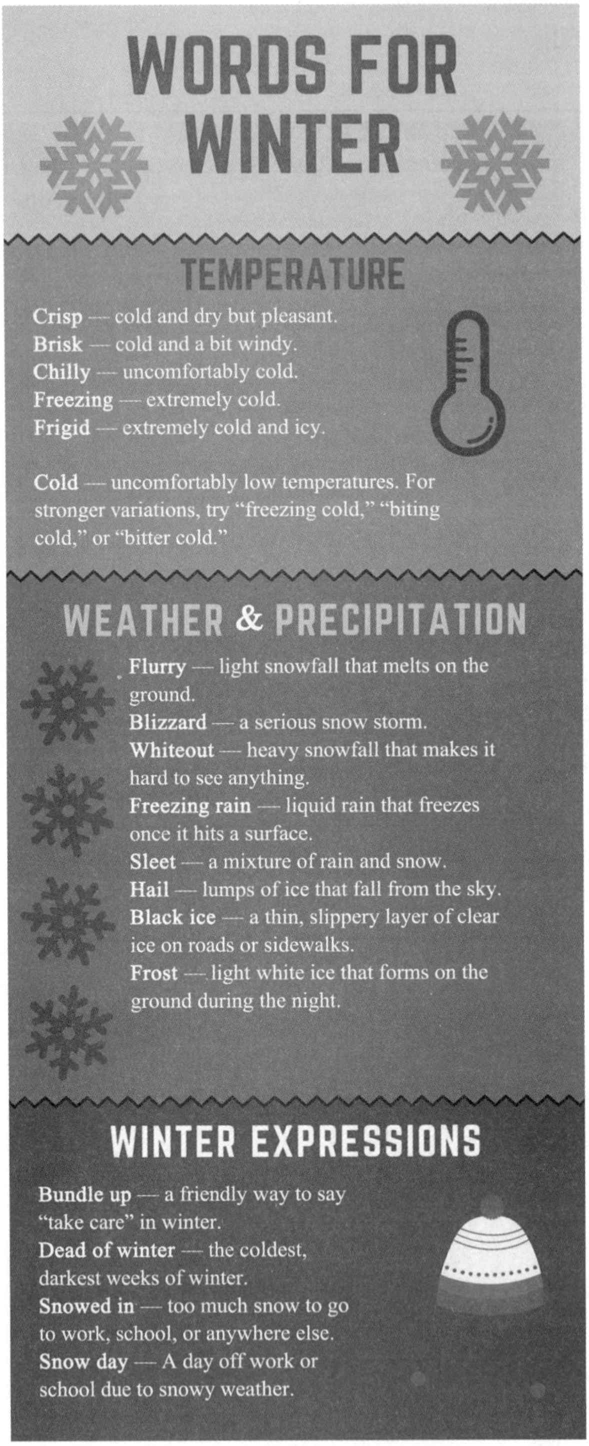

Pic. 4-2 Words for winter

A5. Follow-up Activities

Blank Filling

Complete the following sentences with the words in the box. Then role play.

clear	changeable	frost	fair	extreme

Bob and Andrew are going on a trip and deciding what to take.

Bob: Is the weather going to be good?

Ann: Yes, the meteorologist on television said that it would be hot and dry.

Bob: Yes, it should be ___1___.

Ann: But the weather forecast is normally wrong. Just in case, we'd better prepare for ___2___ weather.

Bob: I also think it might be quite cold at night if the sky is ___3___. We might even get ___4___ in the mornings.

Ann: We should take some warm clothes then.

Bob: And take some umbrellas in case it rains.

Ann: I don't normally go on a trip this early in the spring because the weather is always so ___5___.

Bob: Yes, I know what you mean. It makes packing difficult.

Ann: But no matter how good or bad the weather is we'll have a good time.

Bob: Yes, we will.

(Adapted from *excellentesl 4u.com*)

Conversation Making

Use the weather as your conversation starter and make conversations according to the following situations. You may refer to the expressions below but don't confine yourself to them.

Situation 1:

It is a hot day. You are at the bus stop waiting for the bus. A man is standing next to you.

Situation 2:

It is a cold winter morning after snowing. You are trying to wipe the snow off your car. Your next-door neighbor also comes outside to clean the driveway.

Situation 3:

You are on your way home. Suddenly a gale starts to blow. Soon the rain is pouring down. You panic and run into the nearest shop for shelter. There are several people in the shop.

Suggested Expressions:

It's nice and warm today.
It's pretty hot, isn't it?
We're having a heatwave!
It's so hot. It must be over 80.
It's nice in the sun.
The weather's lovely.
It's a lovely day.
It's absolutely boiling!
It's positively tropical today.
So hot for this time of year.
I heard it's going to be sunny tomorrow.
We couldn't ask for a nicer day, could we?
Beautiful day, isn't it?
It's freezing outside!
It's a bit chilly. Wrap up warm.
It's arctic out here.
You can see your breath in the air.
It's below zero.
It's pretty frosty today.
My car is iced up.
It looks like raining.
We'd better run for it.
It's only a shower.
It's pouring.
It's bucketing down.
It's been raining all day.
I'm soaked to the skin.
I'm drenched.
Did you get caught in the rain?
Can you believe all of this rain we've been having?
I hear they're calling for thunderstorms all weekend.

(Adapted from *eslbuzz.com*)

Question and Answer

Take turns to ask each other the two sets of questions. Give long answers to each question.

Set 1

- What is your favorite type of weather?
- What was the weather like yesterday?
- What type of weather is most fun?
- When was the last time it rained?
- Would you like to be a meteorologist, and why?

Set 2

- What type of weather do you dislike?
- What do you think the weather will be like next week?
- Do you like going outside when the weather is bad?
- Have you ever seen snow, and what was it like?
- Are meteorologists good at forecasting the weather?

(Adapted from *excellentesl 4u.com*)

Presentation

Please give a presentation on the topic — **the weather in my hometown.**
You may mention the following aspects:

- what the weather is like in general;
- your favorite / least favorite weather and why;
- the most typical weather;
- different features in different seasons.

You may refer to the expressions below but don't confine yourself to them.

Suggested Expressions:

The weather is warmer and often wetter.
Snow is melting along with increased rainfall.
Seeds take root and vegetation begins to grow.
All the trees and plants are in bloom.
Plants may begin to grow dormant.
The birds start singing sweet songs.
The trees bring new leaves on their branches.
Swarms of bees rush at the flowers.
Colorful butterflies fly up in the air.
Heat waves or droughts may cause trouble.
Rainfall may increase in some areas.
Forest fires may become more frequent.
Leaves are falling off trees.

The birds migrate southward.
The weather is cool.
Winter always brings a chill.
You may experience snow or ice.
A white layer of snow covers the ground.
Children love making snowman.

(Adapted from *livescience.com*)

Interpretation

Interpret the following paragraphs into English with what you have learned in Part A.

Paragraph 1

来到异国他乡,首先要适应的是当地的气候。Annie 的家乡是一个海滨小城,气候宜人,冬天也不冷。现在她所在的美国中部的这座小城,是一个四季分明的地方。春天是一年开始的季节,一切都变得生机勃勃,Annie 在家时最喜欢春天了。可是这里的春天完全不同,是一年中气温变化幅度最大的时期,所以要及时关注天气预报。尤其在下着小雨的早晨,会感到格外地清冷。除此之外,春天空气干燥,多大风天气。刮大风的时候,Annie 会尽量避免出门,不然会举步维艰。

Paragraph 2

夏天是一年中气温最高的季节。三伏天是最热的一段时间,太阳炙烤着大地,在户外劳作的人很容易中暑。此外,夏季雨水充沛,经常会下雷阵雨。太阳雨也是夏天常见的景象。如果遇上瓢泼大雨,在外面的人应该尽快回家,因为有时候大暴雨会带来洪涝灾害。高温和雨水使天气变得闷热,这就是我们常说的桑拿天。

A6. Extension

Synonym Discrimination

Can you figure out the differences among the words below?
Group 1: humid / wet / damp / moist
Group 2: fog / mist / haze / smog
Group 3: cloudy / overcast

Extensive Reading

Passage One

20 Fascinating Facts about Weather

Our lives are greatly affected by the weather. No wonder weather forecast is such a hit on TV. But do you know the most exciting facts about the weather? Like which place receives the most rain or what is the lowest temperature ever recorded? Read all the amazing weather and climate facts below.

Interesting weather facts list:

- The naming of hurricanes and tropical storms officially began in 1953.
- The wind doesn't make a sound until it blows against an object.
- Average global temperature is up 0.94°C (1.7°F) since 1880.
- Fire whirls are tornadoes made of fire caused by wildfires.
- At any given time, on average there are about 1,800 thunderstorms occurring on Earth with 100 lightning strikes per second.
- For each minute of the day, 1 billion tonnes of rain falls on the Earth.
- A molecule of water will stay in the Earth's atmosphere for an average duration of 10-12 days.
- Every second around 100 lightning bolts strike the Earth.
- The fastest speed a falling raindrop can hit you is 18 mph.
- It was so cold in 1684 that the Thames River in England froze solid for two months.
- 9 out of 10 lightnings strike land rather than water.
- Mawsynram in Meghalaya, India is the wettest place on Earth with an annual rainfall of more than 11 meters.
- Highest Temperature Recorded on Earth is 56.7°C (134°F) at Greenland Ranch in Death Valley, California, on July 10, 1913.
- Lowest Temperature Recorded on Earth is -89.2°C (-128.5°F) at Vostok, Antarctica on July 21, 1983.
- A cubic mile of ordinary fog contains less than a gallon of water.
- In 1899, it was so cold that the Mississippi river froze over its entire length.
- The air located around a lightning bolt is heated to around 30,000°C. This is 5 times hotter than the surface of the sun.
- The average width of a tornado's funnel averages about 100 to 200 yards, but it may be as wide as a mile.
- Snowflakes falling at 2-4 mph can take up to 1 hour to reach the ground.
- The country most affected by tornadoes is the USA which faces on average 1,200 tornadoes every year.
- Commonwealth Bay, Antarctica is the windiest place on Earth with winds of 200 mph have been recorded.

(Adapted from *funfactsabout.net*)

Passage Two

What To Do During Severe Weather and Other Emergencies

An emergency can happen anywhere and anytime and it can happen to you. In an emergency situation, it is vital to think clearly and react quickly. If an emergency occurs, it is essential for you to know what to do and what not to do. The time to find this out is before an emergency happens. Once an emergency occurs, do not panic. Emergency information will be broadcast on the Emergency Alert System, it is up to you to determine what action is appropriate.

Here are a few of the differently types of emergency situations you could encounter along with general precautions and safety measures you should follow.

THUNDERSTORMS

Thunderstorms produce many dangerous and severe forms of weather. Lightning, destructive winds, heavy rain and hail can all be products of thunderstorms.

What to do

- If you are outside, get into a building, car or bus.
- If you are in the woods, pick a low area under small trees.
- If you are swimming or boating, get out of the water immediately and onto land as soon as possible.
- If you are in an open area, head for low ground such as a valley or ravine, or crouch down.
- If golfing, leave the course as soon as possible and take shelter in the clubhouse.

What not to do

- Do not touch metallic objects such as bicycles, fences, golf clubs, and equipment such as lawnmowers.
- Do not go near trees, poles, hills, clotheslines, overhead wires, metal pipes, or water.
- If in a group, do not huddle — but spread out.
- Do not use the telephone except in an emergency.
- Do not take a shower or bath.

TORNADOES

Tornadoes are violent storms with spiraling high-speed winds. Tornadoes are usually accompanied by hail, severe thunderstorms and wind. The noise of a tornado has been described as a roaring sound — like a train far away.

When a tornado threatens, immediate action can save your life!

- Stay away from windows, doors and outside walls. Protect your head.
- In homes and small buildings, go to the basement or to an interior part of the lowest level — take shelter in closets, bathrooms or interior halls away from windows. Get under something sturdy or lie in the bathtub and cover yourself with a blanket.
- In schools, nursing homes, hospitals, factories, shopping centers and malls, go to pre-designated shelter areas. Interior hallways on the lowest levels are best. Stay away from exterior glass doors.
- In high-rise buildings, go to interior, small rooms or hallways on the lowest floor possible with no windows. If you can see outside, you are not safe.
- In vehicles or mobile homes, vacate and go to a substantial structure. If there is no shelter nearby, lie flat in the nearest ditch, ravine or culvert with your hands shielding your head and neck.

BLIZZARDS

Blizzards, heavy snows, ice storms, freezing rain, or sleet can be serious hazards. The first line of protection is to keep informed of weather conditions in the surrounding area through weather bulletins.

What to do

- Check battery-powered equipment, heating, fuel, food stock, and other vital supplies.
- Layers of protective clothing are more effective and efficient than a single layer of thick clothing.
- Mittens are warmer than gloves.
- Cover the mouth to protect lungs from excessively cold air.
- Keep your car "winterized." Maintain a full tank of gasoline to keep moisture out of the tank.
- Carry a winter kit containing equipment to help keep you warm, visible, and alive if you are trapped in a winter storm.
- If a blizzard traps you in your car, avoid overexertion and exposure, turn on the dome light at night, and don't panic.

What not to do

- Do not overexert yourself shoveling snow. It is extremely hard work and can bring on a heart attack — a major cause of death during and after winter storms.
- Do not take unnecessary trips.

FLASH FLOODS

In many regions flash floods can strike with little or no warning. Local rains may be so intense that small creeks and streams are unable to accommodate so much water. Storm drains and culverts may turn into raging bodies of water. The force of one foot of swiftly moving water can knock people off their feet.

Observe these flash flood safety rules — they could save your life!

- Keep alert for signs of rain (thunder and lightning), both where you are and upstream.
- Be especially cautious at night. It's harder to recognize the danger.
- Stay away from open channels, ditches and culverts.
- Watch out for rising water levels and do not try to drive through areas with 12 inches or more of water. Be careful of bridges and dips in the road.
- Abandon your vehicle if water begins to rise over the road and head for higher ground immediately.

(Adapted from *wave 3.com*)

Part B Transportation

B1. Introduction

Urban Mobility and Its Evolution

Americans are on the go more than they have been in nearly a decade, due in large part to the economic recovery and the unemployment decrease in the United States. More people are back to work and receiving steady paychecks, which means that we are taking more vacations and venturing on more road trips than we have since 2008.

Urban areas are the most complex settings in which the mobility of passengers and freight is taking place. In several instances, passengers and freight movements are complementary, but sometimes they may be competing for the usage of available land and transport infrastructures:

- **Collective Transportation (public transit).** The purpose of collective transportation is to provide publicly accessible mobility over specific parts of a city. The systems are usually owned and operated by an agency, and access is open to all as long as a fare is paid; the reason why they are called public transit. The efficiency of public transit systems is based upon transporting large numbers of people and achieving economies of scale. It includes modes such as tramways, buses, trains, subways, and ferries.
- **Individual Transportation.** Includes any mode where mobility is the outcome of a personal choice and means such as the automobile, walking, cycling, or the motorcycle. Most people walk to satisfy their basic mobility, but this number varies according to the city being considered. Some forms of individual mobility could be favored, while others could be impaired. For instance, walking accounts for 88% of all movements within Tokyo's central area, while this figure is only 3% for Los Angeles. The density and design of the former are more accommodating to the individual mobility of pedestrians than the latter.
- **Freight Transportation.** Since cities are dominant centers of production and consumption, urban activities are accompanied by large movements of freight. These movements are mostly characterized by delivery trucks moving between industries, distribution centers, warehouses, and retail activities as well as from major terminals such as ports, railyards, distribution centers, and airports. The growth of e-commerce has been associated with an increase in the home deliveries of parcels.

The mobility of freight within cities tends to be overlooked but is part of an emerging field related to city logistics.

Rapid urban development occurring across much of the globe increased the mobility of passengers and freight within urban areas. Mobility also tends to involve longer distances, but evidence suggests that commuting times have remained relatively similar over the last hundred years; approximately 1 to 1.2 hours per day is spent on average commuting. This means that commuting has gradually shifted to faster transport modes, and consequently, greater distances could be traveled using the same amount of time.

Each form of urban mobility, be it walking, the automobile, or urban transit, has a level of suitability to fill mobility needs. Different transport technologies and infrastructures have been implemented, resulting in a wide variety of urban transport systems around the world.

(Adapted from *transportgeography.org*)

B2. Words and Expressions

Vocabulary

1. helicopter /ˈheləˌkɑːptə/ *n*. 直升机
2. ferry /ˈferi/ *n*.（尤指定期的）渡船，轮渡
3. cruise /kruːz/ *n*.（豪华）邮轮

Means of Transportation	**交通方式**
car	汽车
truck	（美）卡车
lorry	（英）卡车
bus	公交车
coach	长途大巴
tram	电车
taxi	出租车
airplane	飞机
direct flight	直达航班
airport shuttle bus	机场大巴

helicopter	直升机
train	火车
high-speed train	高铁，动车
subway	(美)地铁
underground / tube	(英)地铁
metro	(法)地铁
transfer station	换乘站
boat	船
ferry	轮渡
cruise	邮轮
motorcycle	摩托车
electric bike	电动自行车
bicycle	自行车
tricycle	三轮车
wheelchair	轮椅

Vocabulary

1. pedestrian /pəˈdestrɪən/ *n.* 行人，步行者
2. intersection /ˌɪntəˈsekʃən/ *n.* 十字路口，交叉路口
3. barricade /berəˈkeɪd/ *n.* 障碍，路障
4. detour /ˈdiːtʊə/ *n.* & *v.* 绕行路线，绕行

Traffic	**交通**
lane	车道
center divider	中央分道线
carpool	拼车
speed limit	限速
speed detection	测速
pedestrian	行人
intersection	十字路口
crosswalk	人行横道
zebra crossing	斑马线
flyover	立交桥

pedestrian overpass	人行天桥
traffic jam / congestion	交通堵塞
bump	减速带
bumper-to-bumper	道路拥堵的
traffic cone	锥形路障
barricade / roadblock	路障
run the red light	闯红灯
overspeed	超速
rear-end	追尾
hit-and-run	肇事逃逸
car crash	撞车
detour	绕行路线
make a U-turn	掉头
parking lot	停车场
sidewalk	人行道
parking meter	停车收费表
tow away	拖走
fine	罚款
ticket	罚单
flat tire	轮胎漏气
driver's license	驾照
learner's permit	驾驶学习执照
The traffic light is on amber.	黄灯亮了。

Vocabulary

1. turnpike /ˈtɜːnpaɪk/ *n*. 收费公路
2. boulevard /ˈbʊləvɑːrd/ *n*. 林荫大道
3. driveway /ˈdraɪvweɪ/ *n*. (沿途有房屋的)路,(街道通往住宅的)车道
4. artery /ˈɑːtəri/ *n*. (指主要公路、河流、铁路线等)干线,要道
5. HOV lane /ˌeɪtʃəuˈviː leɪn/ *n*. 共乘车道或多乘员车道(high-occupancy vehicle 的缩写)

Roads	**道路**
highway	公路，交通要道
interstate highway	州际公路
turnpike	收费公路
toll highway	收费公路
toll-free highway	免费公路
four-lane highway	四车道公路
expressway	（美）高速路，快速路
motorway	（英）高速公路
freeway	（免费的）高速公路
road	道路
street	街道
avenue	大街
drive / driveway	（沿途有房屋的）路，（街道通往住宅的）车道
boulevard	（英）林荫大道
parkway	（美）林荫大道
artery	干线
route	路线
path	小径
back road	小道，僻径
bus lane	公交车道
HOV lane	共乘车道或多乘员车道

Vocabulary

1. ignition /ɪgˈnɪʃən/ *n*. 点火装置，点火器
2. transmission /trænsˈmɪʃən/ *n*. 传动装置
3. gauge /geɪdʒ/ *n*. 测量仪表
4. speedometer /spɪˈdɑːmɪtə/ *n*. 速度计
5. visor /ˈvaɪzə/ *n*. 遮阳板

Inside a Car	**车的内部**
ignition	点火开关
brake pedal	刹车踏板

gas pedal	油门踏板
steering wheel	方向盘
stick shift	档把
automatic transmission	自动挡
emergency brake	手刹
dashboard	仪表盘
diesel gauge	柴油表
speedometer	速度计
wind shield	挡风玻璃
wiper	雨刷
rearview mirror	后视镜
rearview camera	倒车影像
moon roof	天窗
cupholder	杯托
glove compartment	(汽车前座前放小物件的)杂物箱
horn	车喇叭
seat belt	安全带
tighten the seat belt	系好安全带
buckle up	系好(安全带)
emergency light button	应急灯按钮
window power	车窗电源
visor	遮阳板
passenger seat	副驾驶座
driver's seat	驾驶座
car seat for baby	婴儿座椅

Vocabulary

1. exhaust /ɪg'zɑːst/ *n*. (汽车的)尾气,排气管
2. beam /biːm/ *n*. 光束,光柱
3. radiator /'reɪdɪeɪtə/ *n*. 散热器,冷却器

Outside a Car	**车的外部**
door handle	门把手
side mirror	侧方后视镜

car trunk	后备厢
license plate	车牌
gas tank	油箱
fuel the car	给车加油
brake light	刹车灯
indicator light	指示灯
head light	前灯
signal light	方向灯,指示灯,信号灯
fog light	雾灯
exhaust pipe	排气管
spare tire	备用轮胎
hood	车前盖
high / low beam mode	远光/近光模式
radiator grill	散热器栅栏
bumper	保险杠

Vocabulary

1. compact /kəm'pækt/ *adj*. 紧凑的,小巧的
2. inclusive /ɪn'kluːsɪv/ *adj*. (价格或数量)包括一切的
3. theft /θeft/ *n*. 偷窃行为,盗窃

Rent a Car	**租车**
mini car	迷你车型
economy car	经济车型
compact car	紧凑车型
intermediate car	中型轿车
standard car	标准轿车
full size car	全尺寸轿车
premium car	高档轿车
luxury car	豪华轿车
rental agreement	租车协议
rental period	租车期限
road tax	公路税

roadside assistance	道路救援
one way rental	异地还车
grace period	付款优惠期
full prepay	全额预付
delivery	上门送车服务
collection	上门取车服务
basic rate	基本费率
inclusive rate	全包费率
security deposit	押金，保证金
theft protection	防盗险

B3. Situational Conversations

Conversation 1 Travelling to the City

J: Jane A: Andrew P: Patrick

J: Good morning, Andrew.

A: Good morning, Jane. Are you going somewhere?

J: Yes. Patrick and I are going to the city to do some shopping and have lunch.

A: That sounds fun. How will you get there?

P: I want to take the train, but Jane prefers to ride her bicycle.

A: Don't you like using the train, Jane?

J: The train station is far away and riding my bicycle does not cost anything.

P: Ok. Jane, why don't we travel by bus, there is a bus stop just behind the university.

J: It might take longer. I think we will need to take two buses to the city center.

A: Jane is right. There is not a direct bus into the city. Why don't you use a taxi?

P: That will be quick, but expensive. Can you **rollerblade**?

J: I hope you don't mean we should rollerblade to the city.

A: Is rollerblading popular in America, Patrick?

P: Yes. People often use roller-skates. There is even **a designated lane** for it.

J: In the U.K., we can't do that, the path is just for walking on.

A: I need to go to the train station to buy some tickets. I can give you both a lift in my car.

J: That would be wonderful, Andrew. Thank you so much.

P: That is very kind of you, Andrew. Let's go to the city center!

(Adapted from *excellentesl 4u.com*)

☞ **Notes**

- **rollerblade**: to move on a surface wearing a boot with a single row of small wheels on the bottom so that you can travel along quickly for enjoyment.
- **a designated lane**: an officially chosen lane for a specific vehicle to travel on the road and this type of vehicle must travel in this lane.

Conversation 2 Going Back to Thailand

L: Lucy T: Tui

L: What are you doing, Tui?

T: I'm planning my trip back to Thailand for the mid-term break.

L: That sounds exciting.

T: Not really. I must do a lot of travelling to get back to my home.

L: Really? Why? How will you get home and how long will it take?

T: It will take more than 24 hours because I have to use many different types of transport.

L: Will your family meet you at the airport in Thailand?

T: No. I must take a bus from the airport to my home. The bus is very uncomfortable.

L: That does not sound nice. How will you get to London Heathrow Airport?

T: I think it will be cheapest to use the coach, but I have a lot of luggage.

L: That's OK. Usually, you can pay extra to take more luggage.

T: Really? That's good. Do you know where the bus station is from here?

L: Yes, you can walk there. It will only take you 5 minutes.

T: Should I buy a ticket before travelling?

L: Buy your ticket online if you can. It is always cheaper online.

T: I want to travel directly to London. Do they have direct buses to the airport?

L: Yes, it takes about 2 hours.

T: Perfect! I will take the bus. I was thinking about a taxi, but it's expensive.

L: So, when is your flight?

T: Tuesday morning. I need to leave really early as I must check in three hours before.

L: Would you like to take some of my delicious homemade cake for your family?

T: Thanks, Lucy. But I don't think I can. The **customs officer** is usually really strict.

L: I understand. Have a safe journey and see you when you get back.

T: Thanks, Lucy. See you soon!

(Adapted from *excellentesl 4u.com*)

> ☞**Notes**
>
> - **customs officer**: a law enforcement agent who enforces customs laws, on behalf of a government. Their job is to ensure that people who enter or exit the country do so legally, and that they don't bring anything in or take anything out that they shouldn't. A customs officer can work in an airport, at a dock, or any major land port of entry.

Conversation 3 Renting a Car

C: Clerk M: Mary

C: Good morning. May I help you?

M: I'd like to rent a car, please.

C: Okay. Full-size, mid-size or compact, madam?

M: Full-size, please. What's the rate?

C: 78 dollars a day with **unlimited mileage.**

M: And I'd like to have insurance just in case.

C: Is there an additional driver?

M: No.

C: If you want full coverage insurance, it will be 8 dollars per day. It includes **collision damage waiver** and personal accident insurance.

M: All right. I'll take it.

C: Here is our brochure, madam. Err... full-size... OK. Please choose a model in this section.

M: How about this one?

C: All right. How many days would you like to use it?

M: Just one day.

C: May I see your driver's license and credit card please?

M: Is the international driving license fine?

C: Yes, it is. Thank you. Please fill in this form. Can you check this box, and put your initials here, and again here.

(Adapted from *audioenglish.org*)

☞ **Notes**

- **unlimited mileage**: the distance you drive using the rental car is not limited during the rental period. Unlimited mileage car hire is usually slightly more expensive than limited but it can save money if you're taking a long road trip on your rental.
- **collision damage waiver**: an optional service sold by rental car companies to cover you in case of an accident or damage to your rental car. It covers only the rented vehicle and means that the rental company waives its right to pursue you for damage.

B4. Picture Knowledge

Pic. 4-3 British vs. American: transportation

Pic. 4-4 Road signs

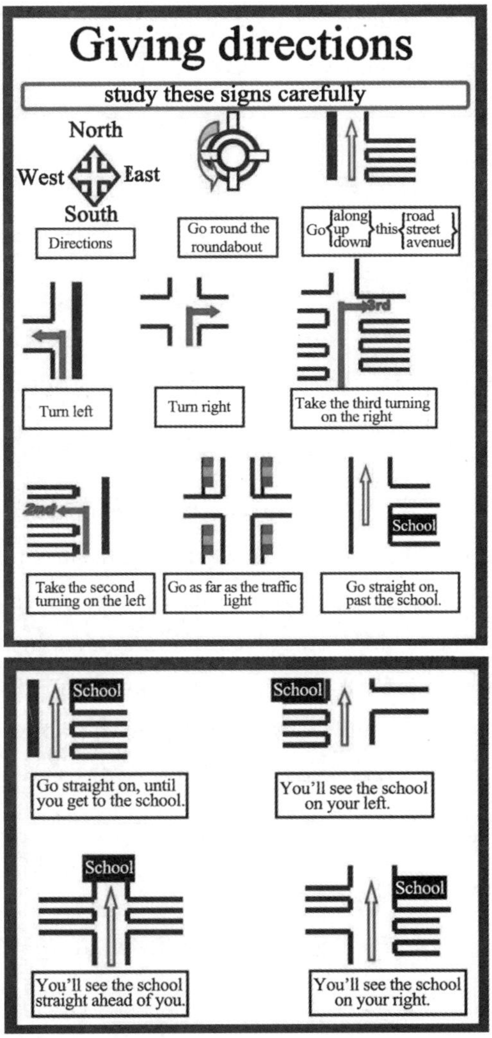

Pic. 4-5 Giving directions

B5. Follow-up Activities

Story Retelling

Read the story below and repeat it to the class with details.

Never Ever Dare to Touch Me Again

A taxi passenger tapped the driver on the shoulder to ask him a question. The driver shouted aloud, the cab got out of control and nearly hit a bus. It went up on the footpath and stopped inches away from a shop window. For a second there was complete silence in the cab, then the driver said, "Sir, don't you ever do that again. You nearly killed me!" The passenger apologized for his tap and said, "Sorry, I didn't know that a little tap would scare you so much. " The cab driver replied, "No, Sir, it's not you. Actually, today is my first day as a cab driver — I used to drive a funeral van for the last 25 years and no one tapped."

(Adapted from *quitpit.com*)

Dialogue

You stay in a dorm for two in the university. When you get to know each other, you want to visit his or her hometown sometime in the future. Now you are telling each other how to get to your home. Try to introduce the route and different means of transportation in details.

Discussion

The summer vacation is coming. You and your friends are planning to go visiting a famous scenic site. The choices for transportation include airplane, high-speed train and driving a rental car. You have different ideas about which means of transportation to take from the city you are staying to the place you are headed. Please conduct a group discussion about the advantages and disadvantages of the above mentioned choices and then make a decision. In the end you are supposed to select a representative to summarize your viewpoints.

Interpretation

Interpret the following paragraphs into English with what you have learned in Part B.

Paragraph 1

我姨妈住在美丽的青岛，她经常热情地邀请我去她家玩儿。我和家人住在武汉，这距离可不近，所以当我终于有时间的时候，我开始详细计划去青岛的路线。两个城市之间有直达高铁和直达飞机。坐高铁的话，需要大约8小时。大部分车次都是早上出发。我家距离高铁站约20公里，可以乘坐公交、地铁或者出租车，而公交和地铁都需要换乘。如果选择坐飞机，大约需要2～2.5小时。航班从早到晚都有，但是早上8:00之前和晚上8:00之后的航班相对来说比较便宜。从我家到机场的距离约36公里，没有公交车可以直达，只能选择地铁或者出租车出行。经过权衡，我最后还是决定选择坐飞机，毕竟旅途时间缩短很多。为了节省开支，我买了早上7:30的航班。到青岛之后，姨妈会开车去机场接我。

Paragraph 2

在姨妈家安顿下来后，我开始计划我的青岛自由行。姨妈白天要上班，所以我的出行需要依赖公共交通。青岛是一座美丽的海滨城市，市内交通以公交车为主。普通车票价1

元，空调车2元。青岛是旅游城市，所以公交车的线路非常适宜观光。很多公交车都是沿海行驶，途径各大景点，可以欣赏海景。如果想要去青岛周边的一些景点游玩，可以乘坐海底隧道公交，十分便捷。当然，如果赶时间的话，出租车是更好的选择，只是费用高一点。如果你的目的地恰好在地铁沿线，一定要选择乘坐地铁，这样不仅省钱，还不会堵车。

B6. Extension

Synonym Discrimination

Can you figure out the differences among the words below?
Group 1: subway / underground / metro / tube
Group 2: road / street / path / way / trail / lane / route
Group 3: ship / boat / ferry / cruise / vessel

Extensive Reading

Road Trip Tips to Help You Get from A to B!

Want to know the trick to heading out on the very best road trip? It's all in the planning! Sure, being spontaneous on any travel adventure is always fun, you never know what surprise is going to be around the corner. However, the careful planning of a road trip — from your route to road trip packing essentials is one of the best ways to make sure you have an amazing and most importantly, relaxing holiday.

So whether you have plans to drive across the US or follow South Africa's Garden Route or Australia's Great Ocean Road, we have compiled a helpful list of top road trip tips to get you ready and set to go on your road trip of a lifetime.

Plan your route

Your road trip plans all start when you map out your route. Mind you, it doesn't have to be exact. Pinpoint your start and finish destinations, then choose a few key stops you want to visit along the way.

It's also worth planning some alternate route options. Just in case you need to make a detour or decide to take a shortcut.

Service and clean your vehicle

Whether you are heading off on your road trip by car or maybe you've been converting your dream bus or van to explore the world in, always remember to give it a service before setting off. Give it a clean too because nobody wants to start an epic road trip in a car full of random junk you've been slowly collecting for the past year.

You want to make sure you have a comfortable drive, both under the hood and inside the car! This shouldn't be such a concern if you are renting a vehicle for your road trip but be sure to check it's in good working order before you set off.

Sign up for roadside rescue

Breaking down on a road trip is nobody's idea of fun but this situation will be a lot less stressful if you have got some roadside rescue in place. If you're traveling in a country you are unfamiliar with it's also worth comparing roadside support companies along with their prices and reviews.

Pack important documents

We're not just talking about your passport and driver's license. Both vehicle, health and travel insurance documents are vital.

Get your gadgets ready

First things first, make sure you pack all the appropriate chargers, cables and adaptors for your gadgets. If you aren't attempting a digital detox on your road trip, you are also going to want to make sure your phone is ready to go with all the appropriate apps installed, Google Maps at the ready and of course a suitable data package for wherever it is you are traveling to.

If you're planning to take a camera to snap some super enviable photos, be sure to pack a spare memory card too.

You may also want to consider purchasing some in-car charging adapters or a portable power bank, particularly if you're going to on the road for a few days with nowhere to keep your gadgets fully charged.

Listen to the music

There's nothing wrong with the radio but it's always worth downloading all your favorite music to your phone ready to blast out on your travels. You could even pack a selection of CDs if you're feeling old school — but either way, make sure you take a look at our ultimate Road Trip Playlist for some amazing driving tracks!

Book any overnight accommodation

Although it's not always going to be a requirement to book accommodation in advance, particularly if you are staying at a motel or camping, if you are heading to a popular destination (like a National Park), it would be a great idea to plan ahead and ensure you have somewhere to stay for the night. It may even help you save money rather than paying last-minute rates.

Depending on your route and ideal stops, we recommend checking booking policies for certain places and look for free cancellations in case your plans change.

Take a map

You'll thank us when all your gadgets fail. Map reading is also fun — a great skill to master.

Also: Download Maps.Me for free offline map usage which even comes with step-by-step directions between two points on your route!

Take some snacks

Essential for snacking emergencies, although don't pig out so much that you have to stop for a nap. It may also be worth packing a cool box for keeping your drinks and snacks cool in destinations.

Make a note of gas stations

Running out of fuel is up there with road trip nightmares and without sounding too much like your parents, having a general idea of how far the next fuel station is — and current gas prices — is never a bad idea.

Safety first

Without going overboard, some absolutely essential kit for any road trip includes:

- First aid kit.
- Vehicle breakdown kit (including jumper cables, water bottles, etc.).
- A flashlight.
- Spare water.

If you are traveling to colder destinations, you may also want to pack:

- A blanket.
- An ice scraper & shovel.

A few safe driving tips

Safe driving will be dictated by the destination and types of roads you travel on, but some general safe driving tips and tricks include:

- Don't drive slowly in the passing lane.
- Don't prevent other vehicles from overtaking.
- Avoid cutting in on others.
- Change lanes correctly when it's safe to do so.
- Don't block intersections.

- Give way to others when pulling out.
- Avoid following too closely to the vehicle in front.
- Don't drink and drive.
- Schedule breaks.
- Be aware of the speed limit(s).
- Don't distract yourself when driving (e.g. using mobile phones).

(Adapted from *maketimetoseetheworld.com*)

Sources of Pictures

Pic. 4-1 Retrieved from *7esl.com*

Pic. 4-2 Retrieved from *worldwidefrontier.com*

Pic. 4-3 Retrieved from *7esl.com*

Pic. 4-4 Retrieved from *me.me*

Pic. 4-5 Retrieved from *en.islcollective.com*

References

How Does Weather Affect Our Life? *UCSB ScienceLine*. Retrieved from http://scienceline.ucsb.edu/getkey.php? key=1059 on July 21st, 2021.

Talk about the Weather at Lunch Time. *Excellent ESL 4U*. Retrieved from https://www.excellentesl4u.com/esl-weather-conversation.html on July 21st, 2021.

First Time to See the Snow. *Excellent ESL 4U*. Retrieved from https://www.excellentesl4u.com/esl-weather-conversation.html on July 21st, 2021.

Talk about Natural Disasters. *Elllo*. Retrieved from https://elllo.org/english/0251/272-Ivan-Hurricane.htm on July 21st, 2021.

ESL Weather Conversation. *Excellent ESL 4U*. Retrieved from https://www.excellentesl4u.com/esl-weather-conversation.html on July 21st, 2021.

Sophia. Useful Phrases Describing the Weather in English. *ESLBuzz*. Retrieved from https://www.eslbuzz.com/speaking-about-the-weather-in-english-2/on July 21st, 2021.

Nola Taylor Redd. (2016). The Four Seasons: Change Marks the Passing of a Year. *Live Science*. Retrieved from https://www.livescience.com/25202-seasons.html.

20 Fascinating Facts about Weather. *Fun Facts About*. Retrieved from https://www.funfactsabout.net/interesting-weather-facts/on July 21st, 2021.

What to Do During Severe Weather and Other Emergencies. *Wave 3News*. Retrieved from https://www.wave3.com/story/494465/what-to-do-during-severe-weather-and-other-emergencies.

Dr. Jean-Paul Rodrigue. Urban Mobility and Its Evolution. *The Geography of Transport Systems*. Retrieved from https://transportgeography.org/contents/chapter8/urban-mobility/ on July 21st, 2021.

Travelling to the City. *Excellent ESL 4U*. Retrieved from https://www.excellentesl4u.com/esl-weather-conversation.html on July 21st, 2021.

Going Back to Thailand. *Excellent ESL 4U*. Retrieved from https://www.excellentesl4u.com/esl-weather-conversation.html on July 21st, 2021.

Renting a Car. *Audio English Org*. Retrieved from https://www.audioenglish.org/english-learning/english_dialogue_car_travel_rent_a_car_1.htm on July 21st, 2021.

Never Ever Dare to Touch Me Again. *QuitPit Short Stories*. Retrieved from https://quitpit.com/taxi-driver-jokes/on July 21st, 2021.

Vicki Garside. (2021). Road Trip Tips to Help You Get from A to B! *Make Time to See the World*. Retrieved from https://maketimetoseetheworld.com/road-trip-tips/.

Unit 5 Leisure Time

Part A Sports

A1. Introduction

Sports and Exercise at Every Age

Robert Rich

We all know that exercise is good for us. But it does more than just improve our physical fitness. It also reduces our risk of getting many diseases, such as cancer, heart disease, or diabetes. It helps reduce stress, helps us sleep better, and it improves our mental health. Because it does so much for us, it is important to exercise no matter what age you are. A lifelong exercise program is the surest way to help you live and thrive into old age.

Children

Many kids get most of the exercise they need just by being kids. They run around, climb and play on a playground, play tag, and do many other activities. Make sure your child has plenty of opportunities to run, jump, and play every day. They should be getting at least 1 hour of physical activity each day.

Teens

A lot of teens get interested in playing sports. This could be for their school or through a recreation program. Encourage their participation so they can be active. If they don't want to play an organized sport, they can ride bikes with friends or play football in the yard. As with younger children, give them opportunities to be active. Teens also need at least 1 hour of physical activity every day.

20s

When you're in your 20s, your body is strong and resilient. This is the perfect time to build a foundation of fitness. Develop exercise as a habit. Make it a regular part of your life. That will make it easier to keep it up as you get older. Play sports with friends, such as tennis or racquetball. Go hiking or biking. Your options are endless. You should try to exercise at least 30 minutes a day, 5 days a week. Remember also that, as you age, you lose muscle and bone strength. So be sure to include strength training as part of your routine now. That way losing a little muscle mass down the road won't hurt you. Aim to include muscle-strengthening exercises in your routine 2 to 3 days a week.

30s

In our 30s, our body first starts to lose muscle because of age. That makes weight training especially important during this time. Join a gym and start lifting weights. Or you can get some resistance bands and look up videos on the internet. Our bones start to weaken as we get older, too. This is a good time to start focusing on bone strengthening. Make sure weight-bearing activities are part of your routine. This could include brisk walking, jogging, or doing yoga. This is also a good time to experiment with different kinds of workouts. Doing something new helps you challenge new muscle groups. It also helps keep your workouts from getting boring. If you normally walk for exercise, try taking an aerobics class. Are you an avid biker? Try swimming or dancing instead. Mix it up to keep things interesting and your workouts well-rounded.

40s

This is the time of your life when it is most important to have an exercise routine. Our bodies naturally start to decline in middle age. Our muscles begin to lose mass and elasticity. This slows our metabolism and makes it easier to gain weight. During this time, both men and women start experiencing dropping hormone levels. This also makes it easier to gain weight, especially around the abdomen. This kind of weight increases your risk of developing health problems. These could include high blood pressure, diabetes, and heart disease. Exercise is the best way to fight all these changes. Keep up with your cardio workouts, 3 to 5 times a week. If you have pain in your joints, switch to low-impact activities. These could include biking or swimming. But keep in mind that weight-bearing activities, such as walking or jumping, are important during this time. They can help you maintain strong bones and fight age-related bone loss. Be sure to keep up your muscle-strengthening routines, as well.

50s

In your 50s, you may start to experience more aches and pains on a daily basis. Don't let this stop you from exercising. Just adapt your exercise program. Low-impact activities such as walking, biking, or swimming generally go easy on your joints. You may also be even sorer after vigorous workouts. Try reducing the intensity and exercise more often instead. During this time, you'll also have to fight your body's natural tendency to curve forward. Strengthen your core by focusing on the muscles in your abdomen and your back. This will help your body stand up straighter and fight the curve.

60s

This is the time when you can start focusing on preventing falls. Continue your aerobic exercise regimen. Try to get 30 minutes of activity 5 times a week. Lift weights or use resistance training 2 to 3 times a week to keep muscles and bones strong. And start working on balance. The National Institutes of Health recommends daily exercises to help you improve and maintain your balance. These include standing on one foot, leg raises, and walking heel to toe. Practice these things now to fight balance problems later on.

70s+

In your 70s and beyond, you need to maintain your strength and flexibility. This will give you more years of being able to function and be independent. Continue getting aerobic exercise every week, whether it be water aerobics, walking, or dancing. Use resistance bands to keep muscles strong. Continue doing balance exercises to keep from falling. Devote extra time to warming up and cooling down so you don't hurt your muscles. And remember to stretch every day to maintain your flexibility.

(Adapted from *familydoctor.org*)

A2. Words and Expressions

Vocabulary

1. relay /ˌrɪˈleɪ/ *n.* 接力赛;转播,转发
2. archery /ˈɑːtʃəri/ *n.* 射箭运动
3. martial arts /ˌmɑːrʃəl ˈɑːrts/ *n.* 武术
4. sprint /sprɪnt/ *n.* 短跑,冲刺

Types of Sports	**运动类型**
competitive sports	竞技体育
non-competitive sports	非竞技体育

spectator sports	观赏性运动
individual sports	个人运动
team sports	团队运动
indoor sports	室内运动
outdoor sports	室外运动
athletics /track-and-field sports	田径运动
ball sports	球类运动
water sports	水上运动
combat sports	格斗运动
gymnastics	体操
relay	接力赛
pole vault	撑竿跳
hurdles	跨栏
figure skating	花样滑冰
short-track speed skating	短道速滑
backstroke	仰泳
breaststroke	蛙泳
weightlifting	举重
wrestling	摔跤
archery	射箭
fencing	击剑
martial arts	武术
diving	跳水
shooting	射击
rings	吊环
sprint	短跑
walking	竞走
marathon	马拉松
floor exercises	自由体操

Vocabulary

1. tournament /ˈtʊənəmənt/ *n.* 锦标赛
2. junkie /ˈdʒʌŋki/ *n.* 上瘾的人
3. squeak /skwiːk/ *v.* 勉强通过,侥幸成功
4. smash /smæʃ/ *v.* 打破,摧毁,粉碎
5. blockbuster /ˈblɑːkbʌstə/ *n.* 非常成功,风靡一时

Matches and Games	体育比赛
away game	客场比赛
home game	主场比赛
host country	主办国
tournament	锦标赛
sports junkie	体育迷
soccer nuts	足球迷
celebrity fans	明星粉丝
conversation starter	开启聊天的话题
high-profile match	备受关注的比赛
watch a live match on TV	观看电视直播比赛
the most watched sports	人们最爱观看的体育运动
take someone to a ball game	带某人去看球赛
score a goal	进球得分
in the playoff	在季后赛
find oneself at a disadvantage	发现自己处于劣势
skip much of the season	错过大部分赛季
on and off the court	在球场内外
qualify for the World Cup	取得世界杯参赛资格
in the knockout stage	在淘汰赛阶段
achieve one's full potential	完全发挥潜能
win a quarter-final	赢得四分之一决赛
squeak out a victory	险胜
beat the ex-world champion	打败前世界冠军
rank the top 25	排名前 25
smash a record	打破纪录
set a world record	创造世界纪录
switch up one's playing style	改变打球风格
top the rankings for a record 100 weeks	连续 100 周蝉联榜首
achieve a Career Grand Slam	实现职业大满贯
make him a living legend	让他成为一个活着的传奇
sign with a club	和俱乐部签约
blockbuster trade	一鸣惊人的交易
earn sb. a spot on the Olympic team	为某人赢得奥运代表队的席位
win Olympic medals	赢得奥运奖牌

rise to fame overnight	一夜成名
become a household name	家喻户晓
declare one's retirement	宣布退役
end one's career on a high note	高调结束职业生涯

Vocabulary

1. indulge /ɪnˈdʌldʒ/ *v.* 沉溺于，使放纵
2. binge /bɪndʒ/ *v.* 无节制地吃喝
3. tone up /toʊn ʌp/ *v.* 使(身体)更强健
4. hone /hoʊn/ *v.* 磨砺，训练
5. abdominal /æbˈdɑːmənəl/ *adj.* 腹部的
6. squat /skwɑːt/ *v.* 蹲坐

Fitness and Workouts	**健康和健身**
hit the gym	去健身房
work out	健身，锻炼身体
regular gym-goer	定期去健身的人
fitness freak	健身狂人
take up regular exercise	经常做运动
loyal regular	忠诚的常客
gym newbie	健身新手
full-body workout	全身健身
light exercise / low-impact exercise	低强度运动
moderate exercise	中强度运动
vigorous exercise / high-impact exercise	高强度运动
fitness instructor / trainer	健身教练
be tailored to your specific need	为你量身定制
custom-made plan	量身定制的计划
hog machine	霸占机器
indulge over the holiday	假期放纵吃喝
binge eating and drinking	暴饮暴食
eat clean	注意饮食

trial session	试听课
pay per visit	单次付费
time trial	时间考验
burn 500 calories	燃烧 500 卡路里
warm up	热身运动
cool down	放松运动，舒缓运动
aerobics	有氧运动
do push-ups	做俯卧撑
do sit-ups	做仰卧起坐
do pull-ups / do chin-ups	做引体向上
do yoga / practice yoga	做瑜伽
do jumping jacks	开合跳
stretch out	伸展
tone up muscles	增强肌肉
hone athletic skills	训练运动技能
weight loss or maintenance	减轻体重，保持体重
keep shape / get in shape	保持体型
get back into shape	恢复体型
prevent aging	预防衰老
ward off diseases	抵御疾病
treadmill	跑步机
rower	划船机
upright bike	立式脚踏车
chest press machine	胸部推举机
abdominal trainer	腹部训练机
sit-up bench	仰卧板
squat rack	深蹲架
stretch strap	弹力带

A3. Situational Conversations

Conversation 1　Going to Sporting Events

D: David　M: Michael

David and Michael are talking about the reasons why people go to sporting events.

D: Sporting events bring numerous fans to games each year. What do you think makes people go to sports?

M: I guess it's more than just the game that draws so many fans into the stands. The live experience, from the smell of hot dogs to the sound of a roaring crowd, is something that you just can't get watching at home.

D: Absolutely! For me, it's more like a socializing event. Maybe it's the common interest in or hatred of a team that starts the conversation, or the simple joy of having a beer with a stranger.

M: **Same here.** It feels great to talk to sports fans and interesting folks seated next to you. Sporting events just bring people together.

D: Another reason might be halftime shows, I suppose. A good halftime show engages the crowd and keeps them happy while the teams are resting up and preparing their second-half strategy.

M: And those shows help you create those special memories. It may even be the thing the attendees will be talking about for years to come.

D: By the way, what's the best halftime show you've ever seen?

M: **Coldplay**'s performance at **the Super Bowl** in 2016. I think that's one of the most top-rated halftime shows over the last 20 years.

D: The musicians must have captivated the audience.

M: You bet it! People are really into those shows.

D: People are also into giveaways! There's always the chance that you could walk away with some cool **swag** like a **jersey**, a badge, a scarf or rally towels.

M: Yeah. If you are lucky, you may even get a chance to win a free VIP package to a future event.

D: That's so appealing to me! People are thrilled at getting something for showing up and attending an event.

M: Yep, that's viewed as part of the game-watching experience. Is there anything else that makes people go to sporting events?

D: Personally, team spirit is another thing that attracts me to the game. All the players are trying to be cooperative and supportive.

M: And the fans are doing the same! When you put fans from opposing teams in the same stadium, there's bound to be a ton of **smack talk**, and, of course, team **camaraderie**. It's the perfect chance for **diehard** fans to show some team pride, painted faces and all.

D: Such a sense of belonging really matters a lot!

M: Anyway, an amazing attendee experience brings people to games.

(Adapted from *eventbrite.com*)

☞ **Notes**

- **"Same here."**: It's said when you agree with what has been said or you have experienced the same thing as they have.
- **Coldplay**: a British rock group whose melodic piano-driven anthems lifted it to the top of the pop music world in the early 21st century.
- **the Super Bowl**: the annual championship game of the U.S. National Football League (NFL), a federation of professional gridiron football teams.
- **swag**: free things that you are given at an event.
- **jersey**: a shirt that is worn by a member of a sports team.
- **smack talk**: critical or insulting comments made to someone, especially an opponent (a person who someone is competing against).
- **camaraderie**: a feeling or friendliness towards people that you work or share an experience with.
- **diehard**: If someone is diehard, he is unwilling to change or give up his ideas or ways of behaving, even when there are good reasons to do so.

Conversation 2 Setting Fitness Goals

A: Amy E: Echo

A: Hey, you look so **buff**! How's everything?

E: Yeah, you know what? I've been going to the fitness club recently. The training really **pays off**. Now I'm in great shape and I know more about how to keep fit.

A: Awesome! Tell me about it. I'm planning to get fitter and slim down for the summer.

E: I'd love to share! First, start small. Setting goals that are actually achievable can help you stay motivated. When you complete your goals, no matter how modest these goals are, it creates this feeling like I can do more.

A: Sounds reasonable. Set achievable goals and stick to them.

E: Then think of starting an exercise routine. Start at the bottom and work your way up. Even short **bouts** of exercise have value, and they can help you build up your fitness level over time.

A: What do you mean by short bouts?

E: Simple exercises that won't take you long, like brisk walking.

A: Brisk walking? You must be kidding me! Does it count as exercise?

E: Brisk walking absolutely counts as exercise, as do a lot of other activities that don't require a sweatband or special **gear**. You don't have to sweat in order to reap health benefits.

A: Great! That suits me well since I'm always too busy to hit a gym. I can walk to my workplace everyday!

E: Great idea! Now let's **bust** some common misconceptions about exercise right here.

A: I'd love to know!

E: You must exercise in 30-minute, uninterrupted stretches. You need to really "feel the burn" or it does not count. They are totally false!

A: Unbelievable!

E: The truth is that you don't have to be a marathoner or a **gym rat** to get meaningful health benefits from exercise. Everything counts when it comes to movement.

A: You are right! By the way, I'm a **huge runner**! I was training for a half marathon last year.

E: A half marathon is 13.1 miles, right? I can't believe you can run that far. I would die!

A: It's a great way to get in shape and it helps me clear my head after a really stressful day.

E: Sounds cool. Run a marathon! Start training for it. That might be a great way to **jump-start** your new fitness goals too!

A: Don't you think that's too much of a jump? I'm not sure whether I will win or lose, but either way, I'll be happy. What else should I do to work on my fitness?

E: Try to **eat clean.** No more fast food, or chocolate, or soda...

A: Oh, stop it! That's too hard for me!

(Adapted from *nia.nih.gov*)

☞**Notes**

- **buff**: If a man is buff, he is in good shape and looks as if he has done a lot of exercise.
- **pay off**: If something you have done pays off, it is successful.
- **bout**: a short period of illness or involvement in an activity.
- **gear**: the equipment, clothes, etc. that you use to do a particular activity.
- **bust**: to break something.
- **gym rat**: someone who spends a high amount of time in the gym.
- **huge runner**: someone who likes running very much.
- **jump-start**: to start or improve something more quickly by giving it extra help.
- **eat clean**: to consume more whole foods — such as fruits, vegetables, lean proteins, whole grains and healthy fats — and limit highly processed snack foods, sweets and other packaged foods.

Conversation 3 Joining a Gym

K: Kevin R: Receptionist T: Trainer

Kevin hits a gym and strikes a conversation with the gym instructor and receptionist trainer.

R: Hello sir, welcome to Fitness Time. How may I help you?

K: My dad and I want to join, but before that we would like to take a tour of the gym. Can we see the gym?

R: Yeah, sure. Let me call someone to give you a tour.

(*After taking the tour...*)

R: How did you like the gym, sir?

K: It is good, spacious and well ventilated. Could you please tell me about the fitness trainers here? Are they all certified?

R: Yes sir. All our trainers are **ACSM** certified. Apart from trainers we also do have helpers on the floor for helping our clients in lifting heavy weights and for re-racking weights after use.

K: That's very good. Could you make me talk to any of your trainers? I just need to ask some questions.

R: With pleasure, sir.

T: Hello sir, I am Max. I am a fitness trainer here. How can I help you?

K: Yeah. I just wanted to know that what kind of training approach is being followed here. I need to put on some pounds as you can see I am so **lanky**. I also want to tone up my muscles and have a **six-pack**. I want to look buff, but I don't want to **bulk up** like a bodybuilder.

T: I see, sir. After you have joined here, you will be informed about complete workout and dietary **regimen** which you will have to follow religiously in order to see some discernible change in your physique. For you, I will suggest at least four days of rigorous weight and strength training followed by just one day of mild-to-moderate cardio and some **abs** exercise. Throughout this bulking phase, you will have to eat like a horse and sleep like a log.

K: Shall I be asked to take supplements later? What are the benefits and ramifications of taking these supplements?

T: Yes sir, but it will depend on you completely whether you want to take them or not. Nobody will force you to take anything. Moreover, we ask only those clients to take protein supplements who are very serious about their physique goals. Protein supplements are essential because the kind of healthy food we eat at home like milk, fruits and green vegetables do not contain all 21-essential-amino-acids. For people who want to put on quality muscle, these protein supplements complete the deficit of protein in their diet. There are no mentionable byproducts of taking these supplements but only if you keep a cap on your daily intake and do not excessively consume them than what has been recommended.

K: Okay. I was also a bit concerned about my dad who will also be joining with me. He is in his 60s and is also an asthmatic patient. What fitness approach would you recommend for him?

T: Sir, we do have Senior Fitness Trainers on floor all the time at our center. They are the ones who basically deal with all elderly people as well as people with any kind of past medical history like heart related, asthma or stroke related. You can bring your dad along without a worry. He will be taken care of properly.

K: Okay. Thanks a lot! Could you tell me about the fee structure or packages that you offer?

T: I am not equipped with all the details about the fee packages. You can ask this at the reception. You will be thoroughly informed.

K: Sure.

R: Welcome back sir. Are you satisfied talking to our trainer?

K: Yes, totally. Could you tell me the fee structure or packages that are available?

R: Yes sir. Here is our manual mentioning all the monthly, quarterly and yearly packaging details. Please go through it.

K: (*after skimming through the manual...*) I have checked it. I would like to join right now and go for an annual package.

(Adapted from *britishcouncil.org*)

☞**Notes**

- **ACSM:** abbreviation for American College of Sports Medicine.
- **lanky:** being tall and thin and often tending to move awkwardly as a result.
- **six-pack:** a set of well-developed muscles on someone's stomach.
- **bulk up:** to make your body bigger and heavier, especially by gaining more muscle.
- **regimen:** a set of rules about food and exercise that someone follows, especially in order to improve your health.
- **abs:** abbreviation for abdominals.

Conversation 4 Working Out at a Gym

J: Jason R: Richard

Jason is a personal trainer at a gym. Richard is working out there for the first time.

J: So, this is your first day?

R: Yep, I think it would be good to take things slowly.

J: We'll see. Let's start with the warm-up, a bit of stretching. Can you touch your toes?

R: This is tough. I can touch my knees.

J: You can do better than that. Can you feel the muscles stretching in your calves — the back of your legs?

R: Yep, getting closer.

J: No, don't **bounce**. Stretch.

R: Alright, but I'm not getting to my toes.

J: No problem. You'll get better with practice. Next, 50 jumping jacks.

R: What?

J: Doing a jumping jack means that you stand with your feet together and arms down, jump up and spread your arms and legs far apart and land, then jump and bring your feet together and arms down again.

R: That's **driving me nuts**!

J: Hold on, please! Now let's move on to the equipment. We'll start in the weight room. Grab one of those dumbbells over there. Let's start with the 5kg weights.

R: Bells?

J: Those weights. The short ones. It's got the weight on the side, see. It says 5kg.

R: Oh yeah.

J: Let's do a few **bicep curls**. Like this. I want to see 10 reps on each arm.

R: Reps?

J: Repetitions come on... one, two...

R: Eight, nine, ten. Pffff...

J: OK. Switch arms.

R: I'm feeling the burn!

J: That's a good start. Two more sets to go.

R: Sets?

J: Yeah, you don't just do 10. You do 10 reps on each arm three times. Three sets.

R: OK.

J: Good job. Take a break. Right, let's move on to the rower. Twenty minutes.

R: The rower?

J: The rowing machine.

R: Ah, I see.

J: Not like that. Keep your back straight. Use your legs not just your arms.

R: Like this?

J: Perfect. Have fun. I'll be back in a bit.

……

J: Finished. Good.

R: Finished?

J: No, we've not finished your workout yet. Let's move onto the treadmill. Set the **incline** to six and the speed to six miles per hour. Thirty minutes.

R: That's fast.

J: You can do it. No, don't hold the handles. Swing your arms.

……

R: OK, right. How do you turn this off? I think it's time to cool down.

(Adapted from *wikihow.com*)

☞**Notes**

- **bounce**: When an object bounces or when you bounce it, it moves upwards from a surface or away from it immediately after hitting it.
- **driving me nuts**: making me crazy or mad.
- **bicep curl**: an exercise in which you bend your arm towards your body at the elbow in order to make your biceps (the large muscle at the front of the upper arm) stronger.
- **incline**: slope.

A4. Picture Knowledge

Pic. 5-1　Sport and exercise

Pic. 5-2 Sport and exercise actions

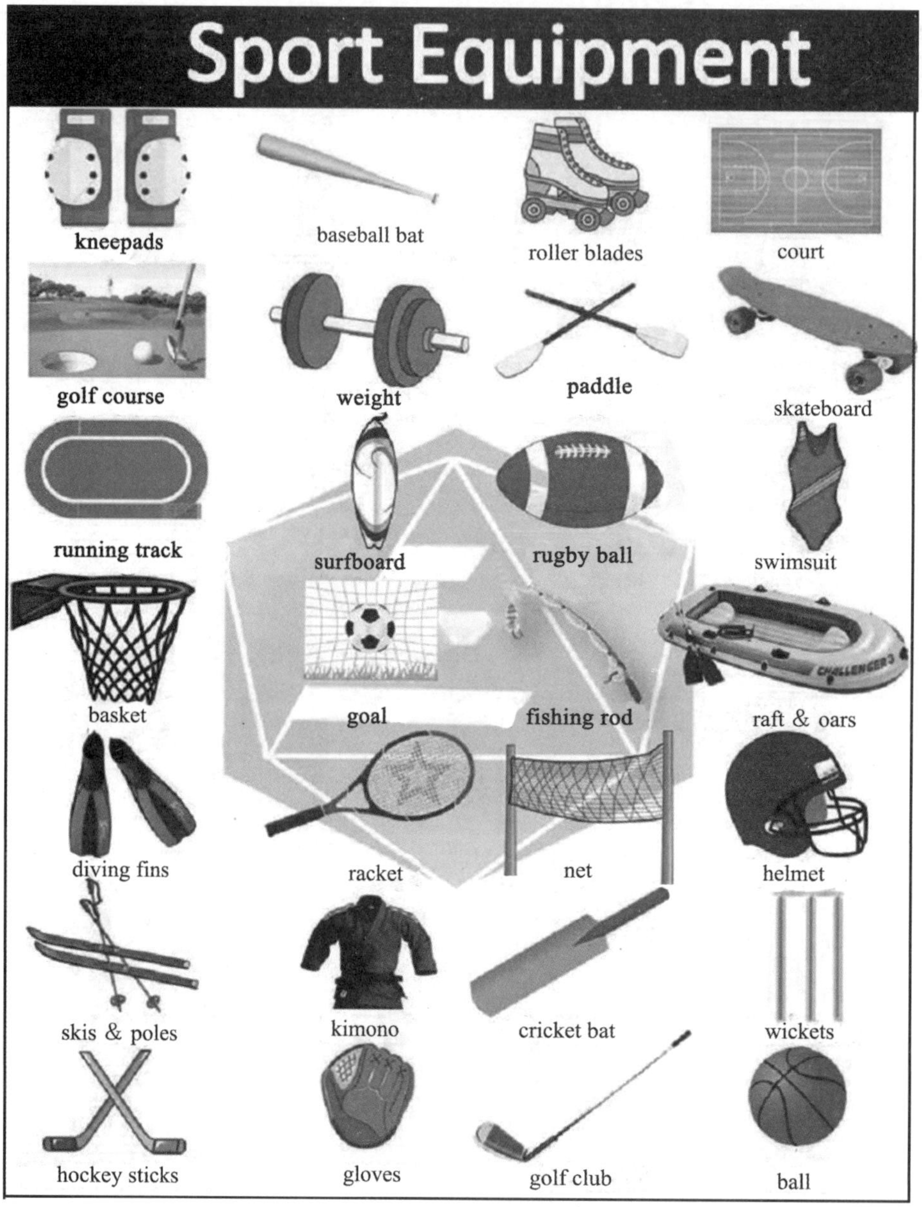

Pic. 5-3　Sport equipment

A5. Follow-up Activities

Blank Filling

Complete the following sentences with the words in the box.

course	circuit	field	court	stadium	pitch	ring	gym	rink	piste

1. The race ________ cuts through the city and out into the country.

2. A basketball ________ has a wooden floor.
3. The golf ________ has eighteen beautiful holes.
4. The soccer ________ is located at the end of this street.
5. How often do you go to the ________ to work out?
6. The players came onto the rugby ________ to begin the match.
7. The boxers got into the ________, shook hands, and began the fight.
8. During the winter, I like to go to the ________ and ice-skate.
9. A ________ is a snow-covered area or track that is suitable for skiing.
10. Thousands of fans packed into the ________ to watch the match.

Presentation

Please give a presentation on the topic — **an exciting competition or sporting event you have witnessed.**

You may mention the following aspects:

- What was the competition?
- When and where did it take place?
- Who won the game?
- Why was it exciting?

You may refer to the expressions below but don't confine yourself to them.

Suggested Expressions:

high-profile match
breathtaking game
once-in-a-lifetime experience
reserve front-row seats
participants and spectators
sports junkie
devoted followers
cheer on an away team
root for one's home team through thick and thin
smack talk
show team pride
all-weather sport
win the coin toss
jersey
score a goal
in the knockout stage
play home / play away
get to the next round
miss a game-winning shot
be placed third in the race
runner-up
rank the top 5
beat the ex-champion
squeak out a victory
burst out in joys
This is happening.

Debate

Critically think about the following topic and hold a team debate.

Is it a good idea to work out with a partner?

You may refer to the expressions below but don't confine yourself to them.

Suggested Expressions:

a matter of personal preference
step foot in gym
work out solo / work out alone
work out with your bestie
work out in a class setting
be 100 percent customized to your needs
conquer your inner couch potato feels
skip an exercise
training partner
enjoy your friend's company
someone in slightly better shape
morning run
social fitness apps
pedometer feature
gym date
no lame excuses
great motivator
pep talk
spur you on
bring out your competitive side
unplug from your daily life
cut the distractions
integrate both fitness and mindfulness
sip on that post-workout coffee
split the cost two ways
social distancing rules
virtual partner
It's a win-win.

Team Work

The box below contains a daily exercise routine for you and your friends. Give it a try first and then have a team discussion.

60 jumping jacks (3 sets of 20 reps)
30 push-ups
20 pull-ups
40 Burpees
50 crunches
40 squats
plank hold, 2 mins.
skip rope, 2 mins.
wall sit, 2 mins.

Your discussion may cover the following aspects:

- Did you manage to complete the routine?

- How long did it take?
- How did you feel?
- What changes would you make to this routine?

You may refer to the expressions below but don't confine yourself to them.

Suggested Expressions:

budget friendly fitness plan	high on my priority list
drop a plan shortly after it begins	stick to my commitment
run a 30-day fitness challenge	stretch my limit
take on the mile-a-day challenge	push beyond my comfort zone
create a weight-loss competition	break through my perceived limitation
score the biggest weight loss	work my ass off
drop some pounds	scale up / dial back the challenge
a ton of fun	set my own schedule
maximize participation	stick with a fitness habit
partner up with fitness-minded pals	one-size-fits-all approach
challenge my workout buddies	reschedule my workout
around the same fitness level	make fully customizable plans
have the same baseline and goal	keep a workout log
stretch goal	track progress in a shared document
beat my squat record	halt progress / reverse progress
hit a new personal best	give a tangible reward
hit milestones	a nice dinner out
surpass someone	home exercise equipment
keep me accountable	You do you.

Interpretation

Interpret the following paragraphs into English with what you have learned in Part A.

Paragraph 1

我是一个铁杆足球迷，尤其喜欢去现场观看足球赛事。不管是主场还是客场，我都会穿上所支持球队的队服，在看台上为他们呐喊助威。最让我难忘的一次现场观赛经历是，在一次世界杯四分之一决赛中，我们国家队在上半场处于劣势，而身为前世界冠军的对方球队则团结合作、打进一球；经过中场休息和战术调整，进入下半场后，我方球员发挥出巨大潜能，在最后五分钟竟然两次射门成功，最终球队以 2:1 险胜。我激动极了，和邻座球迷一起挥舞着国旗！

Paragraph 2

由于暴饮暴食、缺乏运动，我的体重比去年增加了 20 磅。为了恢复好身材，我决定实施一项瘦身计划。首先，注意饮食。坚持健康、均衡的饮食习惯，多吃全天然食品，杜绝加工类和袋装食品，尤其是脂肪含量高的食品。其次，定期健身。我办了一张健身中心的会员卡，每隔一天去一次。在私教的帮助下，运用器械来拉伸身体、增强力量并试图练出六块腹肌。有时，结束了一天的工作，身体非常疲劳，我会在家里做一些低强度运动，比如在跑步机上慢跑或快走一小时。

A6. Extension

Synonym Discrimination

Can you figure out the differences among the words below?

Group 1: apparel / kit / gear / outfit / jersey
Group 2: excited / ecstatic / exhilarated / jazzed

Extensive Reading

All the Sports Words Only Americans Use

Alice. E. M. Underwood

To many Americans, Super Bowl Sunday is synonymous with junk food, cheering, the best new commercials, and possibly the sensation of winning (or losing) a war. People in other countries sometimes wonder if the prize is a very large bowl.

It's not just the fascination with football that befuddles non-Americans — it's the very words we use to describe it. That goes for sports-related words in general, especially when we compare certain terms in American English to their British counterparts.

In other words, a Yank may queue for gridiron and go barmy in the stands as if he's got bugger all to do but watch the match, but lads from Blighty think that's bollocks. And if you don't know what that means, we've got you covered with this handy list of American sports words and their British equivalents. If you just can't get enough football (or if you secretly think words are more interesting), this is the list to get you through the sports event of the year.

General sports words

Sports vs. sport That's right: the language barrier starts with what to call the whole category of athletics. Americans watch sports. British folk watch sport. We've got a lot of ground to cover.

Game vs. match The Super Bowl is also called "the Big Game." We can only assume a British championship would be called "the Oversized Match."

Team vs. club "My favorite football team is the Raiders," says an Oaklander. "My football club is the Gunners," says a Brit rooting for Arsenal (though someone from a rival team might call them "Gooners"). Another British football quirk: many fans call their teams — er, clubs — by nicknames rather than their official titles.

Defense vs. defence It means the same thing: the opposite of "offense" (or if you're in the U.K., "offence"). British English just spells some things differently. (Want more British spelling variations? Learn about *canceled vs. cancelled*, *favorite vs. favorite*, and other ways our Englishes are different.)

Zero-zero vs. nil-nil If both teams have good defense, the score might be zero-zero. But if they have good defence (note the British spelling), then the score will be nil-nil.

Shutout vs. clean sheet In the U.S., a "shutout" is a game in which one team doesn't score at all. In the U.K., the goalkeeper (not goalie) is said to "keep a clean sheet" if he's kept the other team's score at nil.

Tie vs. draw It could be zero-zero, nil-nil, or ten-ten (no changes there); if both teams have the same score at the end of the game, that's called a "tie" for Americans and a "draw" for the British.

Field vs. pitch The thing you play on, if you're playing in the U.S., is a field. In the U.K., it's a pitch — not to be confused by what a baseball pitcher (bowler) throws at a batter (batsman) in the game of baseball (that one's still baseball, though Brits prefer cricket).

Sideline vs. touchline Either type of line designates the boundaries of the field. Idiom bonus: if a player is unable to play, you can say "that player has been sidelined."

Football words

Soccer vs. football When Americans hear "football," we think tackling, touchdowns, oval ball with pointy ends. When Brits (or really, anyone not from the U.S.) hear "football" — sometimes abbreviated to "footy" — they think fancy footwork, goals, round ball. In other words, what Americans call "soccer." Fancy that.

Pig skin This word has no British equivalent. In American football, it's what you call the actual ball. If you didn't know that, "tossing around the pigskin" probably sounds pretty gross.

Gridiron For Americans, a gridiron is the field for football—so called because of the parallel lines marking up the grass. But British folks sometimes use the word "gridiron" to refer to the sport of American football as a whole. It rolls off the tongue nicer than "American football," after all.

In the six In soccer, some American commentators say "in the six" to refer to action in the six-yard box — that is, the area immediately around the goal.

Pick six This term is specific to American football — that is, gridiron. It's what happens when a quarterback throws an interception (or "pick") and the defensive player throws it back, scoring a touchdown worth six points.

On frame This is a football Britishism meaning "on target" — for example, a kick straight into the goal would be "on frame." Americans don't get it: in the words of one Florida-based soccer blogger, "For me it sounds like hitting the post or the crossbar, I wouldn't think it was a shot on target."

Upper 90 vs. top corner In soccer, this term refers to the top portion of the goal. American commentators refer to the right angle as the "upper 90" (as in, 90 degrees), and British ones content themselves with describing the general region.

Sporting equipment

Uniform vs. kit What you wear to show what team (or club) you're on.

Cleats vs. boots (studs) These are what you put on your feet to run in turf. Americans refer to the shoes in general as "cleats," but the actual cleats are the grippy bits on the sole. The grippy bits in British English: "studs."

Sneakers vs. trainers More on footwear: a good running shoe without the studs (or grippy bits) is called a "sneaker" in the U.S.; the British aren't as big on sneaking, so for them, they're called "trainers."

Mouth guard vs. gum shield You'd think that teeth would be more injury-prone. But if you're in Britain, you protect your gums.

Words for the fans

Remember this sentence? "A Yank may queue for gridiron and go barmy in the stands as if he's got bugger all to do but watch the match, but lads from Blighty think that's bollocks." Let's finish translating the Britishisms.

Yank An American. Think "Yankee."

Queue This is what you stand in while you're waiting to get into the stadium. Or the bathroom. Or if you want fries and beer (or at a British match, chips and a pint).

Barmy "Crazy." Not necessarily certifiably insane, just a bit on the loony side.

Bugger all This translates to "nothing at all," but be careful where you say it: it's a bit vulgar as a phrase. You're probably OK saying it on the soccer pitch, though.

Lads Let's not stereotype: there are plenty of lasses (or girls) who are just as excited about a good day of sport. But say you're with a group of fellows. They'd be dudes, guys, or bros in the U.S., but in the U.K., you'd call them "my lads."

Blighty An affectionate term for England herself. The term showed up as a sign of patriotism and homesickness at the time of Victorian rule in India and grew in popularity in the early twentieth century, with songs like "Take Me Back to Dear Old Blighty" causing a tear in many a homesick soldier's eye.

Bollocks "Nonsense!"

A lot of these words might sound like bollocks to American ears, but if you ever find yourself at a footy match in the U.K. — or are trying to explain gridiron to a lad from Blighty — now you'll know where to start. Let the games begin!

(Adapted from *grammarly.com*)

Part B Parties

B1. Introduction

Party Is a Nice Form of Fitting in

When you got your acceptance letter to a university abroad, it opened up the world. You'll soon study in one of the best educational systems and have access to unique opportunities that could launch your career. But it's also a life-changing experience that will make everything new and unknown.

It's normal to be nervous about your big trip, but you won't feel that way forever. Integrating into a new setting with new people is never easy. However, interacting and socializing properly with host nationals help you to better assimilate. You may wonder how? This article aims to help those overseas students who are just finding their feet in a new environment by telling them: party is a nice form of fitting in. It's not just for fun, but more for socializing and conversing.

Let's assume that you, an international student in the U.S., have never been to a party before, but would like to go to one. The problem is you're not quite sure what happens there or what to expect. I'll quickly cover what happens at most parties in this country to take some of the mystery away.

Talking

It can feel like there should be some more exciting, glamorous answers, but parties mainly consist of people mingling and having conversations. They may be doing other things at the same time, but it all hangs off people getting together to talk. Like with anywhere else, the flavor of the conversations can vary depending on who you speak to and what kind of mood they're in. You may chat to one person and do some routine getting-to-know-you small talk. One group conversation may be crude and hectic. Another may be philosophical and intellectual.

Entertaining distractions

Some parties are nothing but conversation, but usually there will be other things to keep everyone entertained. If the party is small enough all the guests might join in. At bigger parties one group may take part, while everyone else does something else.

Here are some common ones: watching a movie, TV show, sports, or online clips; playing a board game, probably a more party-oriented one. Like in between conversations you could have stopped to watch a group playing a video game, or headed to the basement where a movie was on, or gone to the backyard where a few people were trying to get a bonfire going.

A bit of drinking

Not every party has alcohol, but it does appear at the majority of them. That's not to say they're all degenerate booze fests. Even at a more toned-down or sophisticated gathering many of the guests will have a drink or two as they talk.

Some people like drinking for its own sake, and parties are one of the main places where they can do it. For some that means sipping a couple of cocktails over the night. For others it means getting more outgoing, sociable or relaxed.

Of course, none of that means you have to drink much or at all if you don't want to. Just because something is common doesn't mean you have to take part. Lots of people go to parties and either stay sober, or only catch a mild buzz. You can still have fun and enjoy parties for plenty of reasons other than getting loaded.

Now you know what to expect at a party and how you can participate socially there. Going to a party is one of the effective ways for international students to interact with people from both host culture and diverse cultures. It not only helps you gradually integrate into the study, work and life in the country where you stay, but also opens tremendous opportunities for you. One word of caution: Follow the rules and etiquette of partying and socializing in your host country! If not, misunderstanding and uneasiness may easily be caused.

(Adapted from *succeedsocially.com*, *niche.com*, *mdpi.com*)

B2. Words and Expressions

Vocabulary

1. attendee /əˌtenˈdiː/ *n*. 出席者,参加者
2. gatecrash /ˈgeɪtkræʃ/ *v*. 不请自到,擅自参加
3. party pooper /ˈpɑːrtiˌpuːpə/ *n*. 扫兴的人,煞风景的人
4. confetti /kənˈfeti/ *n*. (派对或庆典时抛撒的)五彩纸屑

At the Party	在派对
throw a party / host a party	举办派对
attend a party	参加派对
host / hostess	男主人，女主人
event planner	活动策划人
guest of honor	贵宾
attendee	出席者
partygoer	参加派对的人
gatecrasher	未获邀请而参加者
party animal	热衷于派对的人
party pooper	扫兴的人
the life of the party	派对的灵魂人物，派对上最活跃的人
social butterfly	擅长社交的人
wallflower	桂竹香花，壁花（形容在社交场合因腼腆而不与人交谈的人，即社恐人士）
social anxiety	社交恐惧
social phobia	社交恐惧症
set up the location	布置场地
popper	彩纸爆竹
bunting	彩旗
confetti	五彩纸屑
custom banner	定制横幅
streamer	装饰彩带
set an upbeat mood for the party	为派对营造轻松欢快的气氛
make the location look festive	让场地看起来有节日氛围
play ice-breaker games	玩破冰游戏
buy a cake about this big	买一个约这么大的蛋糕（同时做手势）
enough food to go round	食物足够分给每个人
do the clean-up	清理打扫
give out goody bags	分发小礼品（派对结束或客人离开时送出）

Vocabulary

1. buffet /bəˈfeɪ/ *n.* 自助餐，（车站的）快餐部
2. potluck /ˌpɑːtˈlʌk/ *n.* （参加者各带菜肴分享的）百味餐
3. bachelorette /ˌbætʃələˈret/ *n.* 单身女子
4. slumber /ˈslʌmbər/ *n.* 睡觉

Types of Party	**派对类型**
cold buffet party	自助冷餐派对
theme party	主题派对
potluck party	百味餐
fancy dress party / costume party	化妆派对
welcome party	欢迎派对
farewell party	告别派对
kitchen shower / housewarming party	温居派对,乔迁派对
block party	街区派对
pool party	泳池派对
surprise party	惊喜派对
birthday party	生日派对
baby shower	迎婴派对
graduation party	毕业派对
all-nighter	通宵(派对)
bachelor party / stag night	男性告别单身派对
bachelorette party / hen party	女性告别单身派对
bridal shower	准新娘送礼会
slumber party	睡衣派对(一群孩子都在其中一个孩子家里过夜的聚会)

Vocabulary

1. specialty /ˈspeʃəlti/ *n.* 地方特产,特色菜,专业,专长
2. slather /ˈslæðə/ *v.* 大量涂抹,厚厚涂抹
3. topping /ˈtɑːpɪŋ/ *n.* (浇在食物上的)配料,浇汁(尤指酱汁、奶油等)
4. infuse /ɪnˈfjuːz/ *v.* 充满,注入,泡制
5. simmer /ˈsɪmə/ *v.* (用文火)煨,炖,(分歧或消极情绪)酝酿

Food	**食品**
homemade food	自制食品
store-bought food	店里买的食品

processed food	加工食品
takeout / takeaway	外卖食品(或外卖店)
ready-to-eat	即食的,成品的
staff picks	员工推荐(产品或菜品)
much-loved regional specialties	深受欢迎的地方特色菜
finger food	小点心(可用手抓食)
light snack	小吃
barbecue rib	烧烤肋排
thin-crust pizza / thick-crust pizza	薄皮披萨,厚皮披萨
deep-dish pizza	深盘披萨
crunchy edge	松脆的(饼)边
ketchup	番茄酱
potato chips	炸薯片
French fries	炸薯条
hard-boiled egg	(煮的)全熟鸡蛋
salted egg yolk	咸蛋黄
cheese-baked lobster	芝士焗龙虾
air-dried ham	风干火腿
minced meat	肉末,肉馅
high-grade wheat flour	优质面粉
hand-rolled dough	手工揉的面团
hand-sliced rye bread	手工切片黑麦面包
potatoes layered with onions	土豆夹洋葱片
toast slathered with butter	涂了很多黄油的吐司
cake topping	蛋糕上的配料
rainbow-colored candies	彩虹色糖果
gravy-infused	充满肉汁的
water-simmered	用文火炖的
chocolate-coated	巧克力涂层的,巧克力糖衣的
bread-meat-salad combination	面包、肉和沙拉组合套餐
I'd like a burger to go.	我买一个汉堡打包带走。(非堂食)
I need a doggy bag and a to-go box.	我需要一个打包袋和打包盒。
For here or to go?	堂食还是带走?

Vocabulary

1. fizzy /ˈfɪzi / *adj*. 起泡的
2. mocktail /ˈmɑːkteɪl/ *n*. 无酒精鸡尾酒
3. carbonated /ˈkɑːrbəneɪtɪd / *adj*. (饮料)含二氧化碳的
4. caffeine /ˈkæfiːn/ *n*. 咖啡因,咖啡碱
5. draft /dræft/ *adj*. (饮品等)桶装的,散装的
6. designated /ˌdezɪgneɪtɪd/ *adj*. 指定的
7. neat /niːt/ *adj*. (酒水)纯的,不掺水的

Drinks	**饮品**
alcoholic beverage	酒精饮料
soft drink	软饮料
fizzy drink / sparkling drink	起泡饮料,汽水
carbonated drink	碳酸饮料
energy drink	功能饮料
dairy drink	乳制品饮料
diet drink	低热量饮料
bottled drink	瓶装饮料
freshly-brewed coffee	现煮咖啡
instant coffee	速溶咖啡
cocktail	鸡尾酒
mocktail	无酒精鸡尾酒
herbal tea	花茶
milkshake	奶昔
ready-to-drink	即饮的,成品的
caffeine-free	不含咖啡因的
nutrient-rich	营养丰富的
protein-dense	高蛋白的
low-carb	低碳水化合物的
over-consume calories	摄入过多卡路里
flavorings and sweeteners	调味料和甜味剂
go grab a drink	去喝一杯

happy hour	打折时段(特指酒水)
drink specials	特价饮品
order a drink	点一杯饮品
serve alcohol and liquor	供应酒水
alcohol content	酒精含量
on draft / tap	桶装的,散装的(现酿的)
ice cube	冰块
on the rocks	加冰块的
straight up	不加冰的
at room temperature	室温,常温
propose / make a toast to someone	向某人敬酒
bottoms up / down it	干杯
top up	加满
get a refill	再次添满
legal drinking age	法定饮酒年龄
practice good etiquette	遵守礼仪
designated driver (DD)	指定司机(指一群人中不喝酒并负责开车接送他人的人)
Say when.	够了请告知。(为人斟酒时用词)
Have a neat gin.	来一杯纯的杜松子酒。

Vocabulary

1. hangover /ˈhæŋˌoʊvə/ *n.* 宿醉(大量饮酒后第二天的不适反应)
2. buzzed-up /ˌbʌzdˈʌp/ *adj.* 亢奋的(饮酒过量或滥用药物所致)
3. brawl /brɑːl/ *n.* 斗殴,闹事
4. intoxicated /ɪnˈtɑːksɪkeɪtɪd/ *adj.* 喝醉的

Drinking Misbehaviors	**不当饮酒表现**
excessive alcohol intake	过量酒精摄入
heavy drinking / binge drinking	狂饮,大量饮酒
underage drinking	未成年者饮酒
alcohol abuse / alcoholism	酗酒

growing tolerance to alcohol	增长的酒量
wake up with a hangover	醒来后有宿醉反应
drink someone down	把某人灌醉
drink up... at one breath	一口气喝光
get wasted / bombed/ blind drunk	(喝得)烂醉的
get buzzed-up	变得亢奋
drunken brawl	酒后斗殴
drink-driving	酒后驾驶(英、澳)
drunk driving	酒后驾驶(美)
driving under the influence (DUI)	酒后驾驶(也可指在使用或滥用药物的影响下驾驶)
driving while intoxicated (DWI)	酒后驾驶(接近或等同醉驾)

Vocabulary

1. tab /tæb/ *n*. (代付的)账单,账款,费用
2. gratuity /grəˈtuːəti/ *n*. 小费,赏钱
3. stiff /stɪf/ *v*. 拒付应付的钱
4. split /splɪt/ *v*. 分开,分裂,分摊

Bills and Tips	**账单与小费**
run / start / open a tab	记账,保留账单
put ... on one's tab	把……记在某人账上
pick up the tab / foot the bill	结账
round the bill up	将账目四舍五入为整数(通常上调)
gratuity	小费
leave a good tip / tip big	多给小费
stiff the bartender	不给服务生小费
Keep the change.	别找零了。
This is on me.	我请客。
Let's split the bill.	我们AA制。
We'd like separate bills.	我们单独结账。

B3. Situational Conversations

Conversation 1　Attending a Dinner Party

W: Miss Wang　L: Lucy

Miss Wang is invited to a party. She has never attended one, so she asks Lucy for advice.

W: I've got an invitation from my boss. He is throwing a dinner party in his house. All the people in our department have been invited. What should I do, Lucy?

L: Do you wanna go?

W: Not really. As a newcomer, I don't know many of them.

L: Why not? It's gonna be a fabulous chance to build **rapport** with your colleagues. And you don't want to risk offending your boss?

W: Sounds right. Then what do I need to prepare?

L: Bring a gift for your host. You can't just show up at someone's house empty handed. Some flowers, chocolates or a bottle of wine will be a good choice.

W: I think I'll bring a bunch of flowers.

L: If the party is **BYOB**, you will need to bring your own drinks as well.

W: Oh, I almost forgot! What about the dress code?

L: Well, you don't have to be very formal on such an occasion, but don't be **underdressed.**

W: I see. Is there a specific etiquette that I need to follow during the dinner?

L: Of course. First, when sitting, unfold your napkin and place it on your knee. When eating, if there are several cutlery sets beside the plate, start at the outside of your cutlery and work in.

W: Table manner always makes me nervous. I'm afraid I make mistakes.

L: Never fear. If you're not sure what to do, just have a look to see what the other guests are doing.

W: Can I cool food by blowing onto it?

L: Nope. And don't leave lip-prints on your glass.

W: Alright. Anything else?

L: Don't forget to compliment the food.

W: Okay. It's really hard for an introvert like me to survive a party. Can I just show up for a while?

L: If it is a seated dinner party, you have to stay the entire time. Why not stay longer?

I'm sure you'll enjoy the atmosphere. **Incidentally**, have you ever tried to break the ice in a social setting?

W: No. I'm not sure if I can do that. Any tips?

L: Um, you should look **approachable.** Don't cross your arms. Look open and inviting with a genuine smile.

W: I'm too shy to approach anyone, I suppose.

L: Come on! Just **let your hair down** and **mingle** with other guests.

W: I'll try. What if I still feel trapped at the party?

L: Then you'll have to figure out an escape plan ahead.

W: That makes sense.

L: Just a word of caution. If you drink alcoholic beverages, do it moderately.

W: I'll **go easy on** the alcohol. Thanks a lot, Lucy!

L: **Anytime.**

(Adapted from *millennialmagazine.com*)

☞ **Notes**

- **rapport**: a good understanding of someone and an ability to communicate well with them.
- **BYOB**: abbreviation for "bring your own bottle"; used on a party invitation to request that guests bring their own alcoholic drinks.
- **underdressed**: wearing clothes that are not attractive or formal enough for a particular occasion.
- **incidentally**: used before saying something that is not as important as the main subject of conversation, but is connected to it in some way.
- **approachable**: friendly and easy to talk to.
- **let your hair down**: to allow yourself to behave more freely than usual and enjoy yourself.
- **mingle**: to move around and talk to other people at a social event.
- **go easy on**: not to use too much of something.
- **"Anytime."**: You are welcome.

Conversation 2 Throwing a Surprise Party

K: Kelly L: Lisa

L: Kelly, how did you like your birthday party last night?

K: It was **rocking!** Thank you so much for organizing my surprise party. It was the first time I had a birthday party like that with all my family and friends in probably about ten years.

L: I'm glad you enjoyed it.

K: It was awesome to have everyone out for it. Good company and good food. That Mexican **taco** was my favorite. Who made that?

L: It was me.

K: It was you? **Bravo**! To be honest, I don't think you look like the cooking type.

L: Hah!

K: The set-up of the party was impressive too. It was so festive with beautiful streamers and twinkly lights.

L: Yeah, Frank helped me set up the location the day before your birthday.

K: You're so nice.

L: Frank also made the playlist. Were you happy with the music?

K: Absolutely! He started with softer sounds and **cranked up** the volume with some upbeat music as the party progressed. I just loved it!

L: He really **knows the ropes**.

K: Lisa, **how come** you did all the secret planning without leaking a single word?

L: Well, we've got to be sneaky and make sure everyone was on the same page.

K: Except me! The whole plan was well thought-out! You even picked the restaurant I **frequent** to avoid suspicion.

L: You got it.

K: When you guys yelled "surprise" and I saw my name on the cake, I was so ecstatic! That's the best party I've ever had.

L: We all **had a whale of time**. By the way, how would you like to celebrate the next birthday?

K: It's still one year away! My birthday will land on a Saturday next year. So we may meet up over the weekend, go out for some drinks and maybe a little bit of dancing.

L: Sounds like a great plan.

(Adapted from *wikihow.com*)

☞ **Notes**

- **rocking**: If something rocks, it is great. (slang)
- **taco**: a hard, folded tortilla (thin flat bread) filled with meat, cheese, etc. and often a hot, spicy sauce.
- **bravo**: used to express your appreciation when someone, especially a performer, has done something well.
- **crank up**: to increase or improve something.
- **know the ropes**: to be familiar with a place or organization and able to act effectively within it.
- **how come**: used to ask how or why something has happened.
- **frequent**: to visit a particular place often.
- **had a whale of time**: to enjoy oneself very much.

Conversation 3 British Pub Culture

K: Kevin R: Mr. Rong

Kevin, a native Englishman, is chatting with his Chinese friend Mr. Rong.

K: Do you know pubs have been around for over a thousand years in the U.K.?

R: Incredible! There aren't many things more British than "the pub".

K: Definitely. It is something you should experience if you want to learn about Brits and our culture, even if you don't drink alcohol.

R: By the way, what do pubs serve?

K: If you're a drinker, the usual order at a pub consists of lager, ale, bitter and spirits. If you're not a drinker or you're the designated driver, then you can easily order a soft drink.

R: Could you tell me how to order drinks at a pub?

K: You need to order your drink at the bar, so don't wait around for someone to take your order from your table.

R: So there is no table service?

K: You are right! The bartenders will most likely say "what are you having" or "what can I get you" and you give them your order.

R: "I'd like a beer, please."

K: Uh oh, things could go horribly wrong here. In the U.K., "beer" is an **umbrella term** that can include lagers, ales, stouts, wheat beers... you **get the picture**.

R: How should I respond instead?

K: People never just order "a beer" in an English pub. The tradition is to indicate both the volume, a **pint** or a half, and the specific beer you want. The English usually order "a pint" at a time.

R: "A pint of lager, please." Is that right?

K: Yep! Well in the U.K., it's somewhat traditional to buy a round for people.

R: Does that mean buying a drink for your drinking mates?

K: Yeah, one person buys drinks for everyone in the group; then a second person buys drinks for everyone, and so on. That's why we call it a round.

R: Interesting! Do you tip bar staff?

K: No, we don't normally leave a tip at a pub. If you want to say thanks, then offer to buy them a drink. They can then choose to accept the drink or take the value of it in the form of a tip. You are supposed to tip only when there's a waiter or waitress, say, in a restaurant.

R: I got it. That's for table service. Is it normal to start a conversation with a stranger there?

K: Yeah, you can strike up a conversation with a stranger and even make new friends. You may even get a drink bought for you, but remember to return the gesture.

R: Sounds like fun. I guess that's one of the greatest things about the pub. Let's **go grab a drink** in your **local**!

K: I'd love to!

(Adapted from *greatbritishmag.co.uk*)

☞**Notes**

- **umbrella term**: a term used to cover a group of concepts that all fall under a specific item.
- **get the picture**: to understand.
- **pint**: a measure for liquid equal to about half a litre.
- **go grab a drink**: to go for a drink.
- **local**: a pub near to where a person lives, especially if he or she often goes there for a drink.

B4. Picture Knowledge

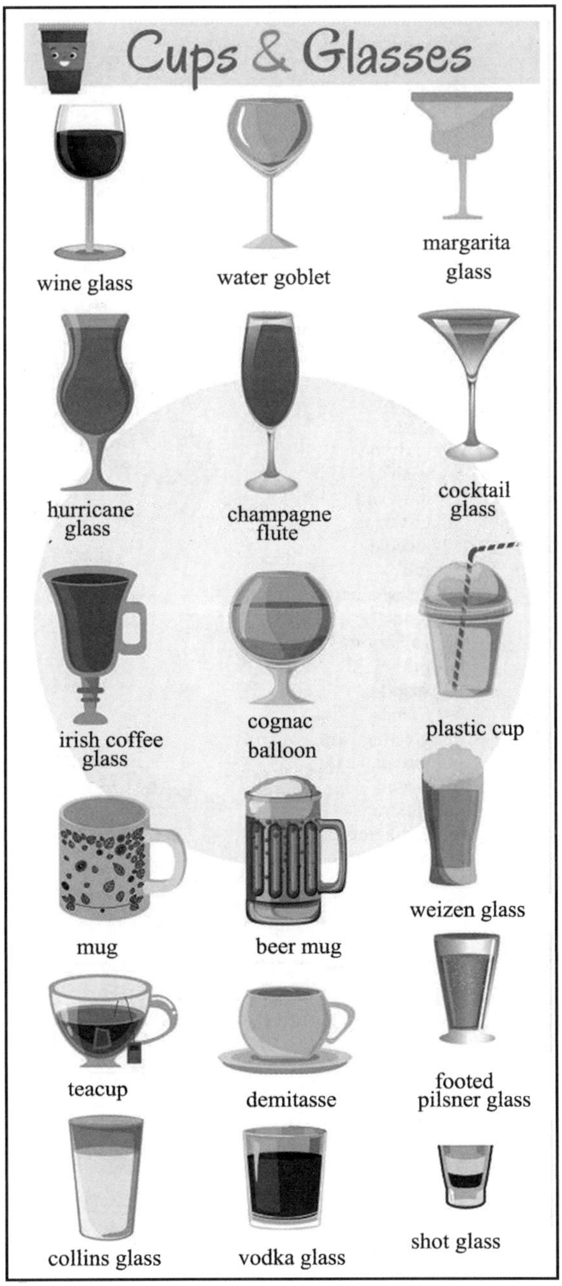

Pic. 5-4 Cups & glasses

Pic. 5-5　Birthday words

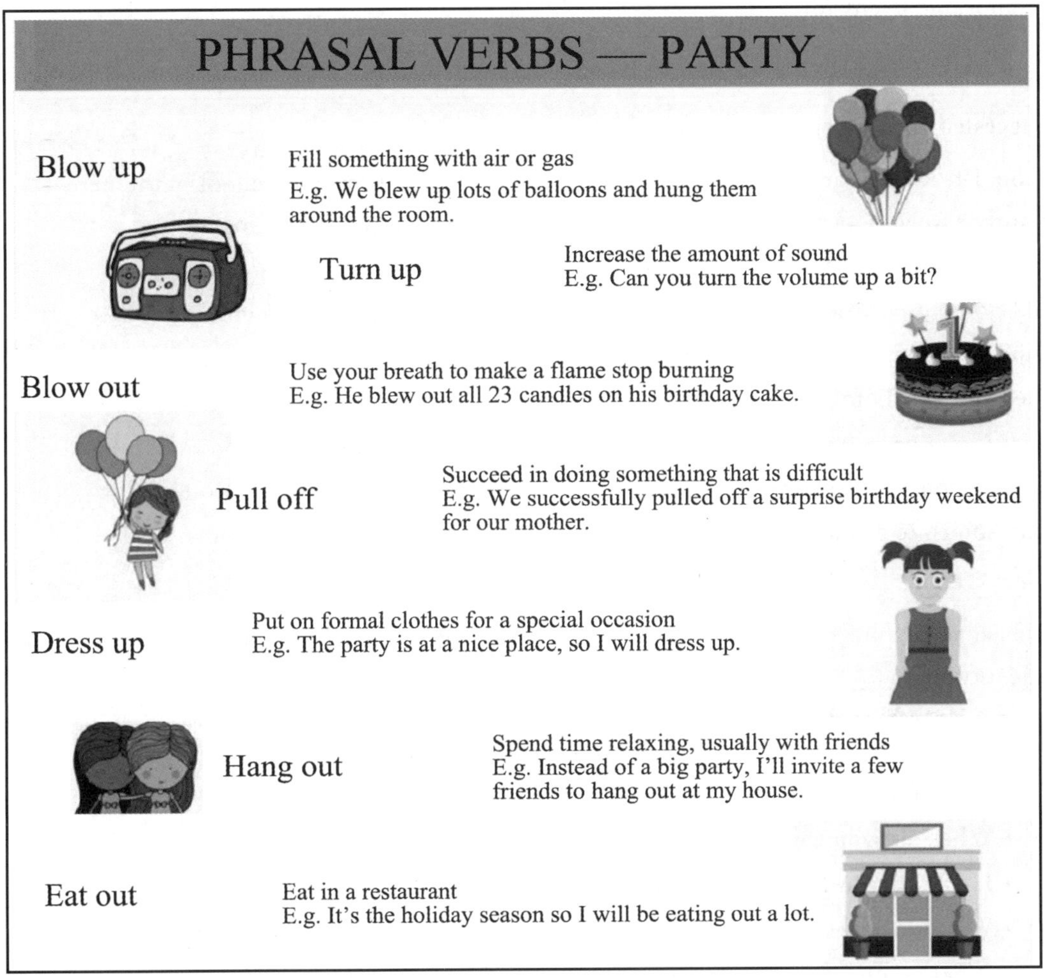

Pic. 5-6 Phrases verbs for a party

B5. Follow-up Activities

Free Talk

A farewell party is generally hosted when an individual (or a group of people) is leaving a certain place for education, work, or any other long-term purposes. The party is a means to bid the leaving person goodbye in a cheerful and happy way, and also convey the message that he will be missed and remembered. A farewell party can be a casual affair hosted in one's house, or it can be a trip, or it can also be held at a restaurant.

Please describe a farewell party that you once attended. You may talk about the attendees, venue, decorations, celebrations, food and drinks, and why it was a memorable event for you.

You may refer to the expressions below but don't confine yourself to them.

Suggested Expressions:

school farewell party
family farewell party
office farewell party
bid goodbye to the going-away person
fond and unforgettable memories
memorable photos and clips
party hats or trumpets
engrave one's name on the memento
gift someone a token of appreciation
a gift with the school emblem
eating preferences
finger food and quick desserts
mocktails and beverages
pop a can of coke
raise a toast for someone
freshen up the mood
wish someone good luck
good luck for the journey ahead

Story Telling

Please tell your own story based on the following scenario and its corresponding questions.

Family Reunion Party

- How did you celebrate your last family reunion?
- What did you eat and drink at the reunion party?
- How did you feel at the reunion party?
- What does the reunion party mean to you?
- What's your plan for the next reunion party?

Team Discussion

You are going to throw a surprise birthday party for your flatmate. Please discuss with the other two flatmates who will help you with the party planning and preparations. Your discussion may cover the following aspects:

- time, venue and budget
- guest list and invitations
- theme and dress code
- food and drinks
- music and games

You may refer to the expressions below but don't confine yourself to them.

Suggested Expressions:

throw a party on a budget
play monopoly

small gathering
guest of honor
organize the big reveal
pick a time
keep one's schedule clear
re-confirm with attendees
cartoon-themed
vegetarian friendly
finger food
paper plates
non-alcoholic drinks
make a playlist
set up the location
do the clean-up
sneaky plan
blab the secret
get right on it
during the pandemic
be extra cautious of
social distance
abide by local public health guidelines
reduce the risk of infection
Get people jazzed.
The party rocks.

Interpretation

Interpret the following paragraphs into English with what you have learned in Part B.

Paragraph 1

留学生可借助有益的社交活动，如参加同学聚会或大学社团，来帮助自己尽快融入当地文化和生活，但一定注意人身安全并遵守当地法律和习俗。首先，懂得保护个人隐私，尤其是银行账户、护照信息等。其次，参加聚会，要有可靠的朋友在身边，提醒自己和他人不要过度饮酒。再次，保持手机畅通并及时与家人或朋友分享行程。最后，聚会结束后，尽可能与好友一起回家并选择安全可靠的代步工具，切记不要酒后驾驶。除此之外，留学生还需了解所在国家对最低合法饮酒年龄的法律规定，以避免不必要的麻烦。

Paragraph 2

上周末，Gordon 教授在家里举办了新年派对。我和几位学长应邀参加，我们都在他所负责的实验室工作和学习。派对当天，我正装赴宴，还准备了一束鲜花和一把中国传统折扇作为礼物送给主人。这是一场自助冷餐派对，室内被彩带和气球装饰得颇具节日氛围。餐桌上摆放了多种冷食、饮品和餐具，还有 Gordon 夫人自制的营养丰富的低热量点心。用餐者没有固定座位，可以随意走动取食，大家边吃边聊，从学术聊到思乡。派对中有专人负责菜肴和饮品的添加及更换；我则自告奋勇充当 DJ，播放了几首新年主题的中英文歌曲。派对结束时，Gordon 夫妇为每人分发了小礼品，并送上新年祝福。

B6. Extension

Synonym Discrimination

Can you figure out the differences among the words below?

Group 1: tipsy / dizzy / buzzed / loaded / wasted / plastered / hammered
Group 2: alcohol / liquor / spirit / drink / beverage

Extensive Reading

Party Invitation Messages

Arlin Cuncic

Throwing a party every now and then is very common nowadays. When you are hosting a party, the first thing you really need to know is how to invite your friends and loved ones to that. Most importantly you need to know what to write in a party invitation message or party invitation card. You need to choose your words very carefully because the words you use in your invitation messages of cards matter a lot. We have here some perfect sample messages about how to invite people to your party. These are the messages you must have a good look at right now!

Invitation messages for party

Having you at the party will be a great pleasure for me. I hope you'll have the time to be with us on [date]. Looking forward to seeing you!

We have decided to throw a joyful party on [date]. You are cordially invited to share the joy with us. Your presence means a lot to us!

Having a guest like you at our party will be awesome. Please join us as we all celebrate the evening of [date] with friends and well-wishers!

A surprise party will be arranged on [date] at our house. We want you to be there just at the right time because you are the most special of all.

You're the soul of any party, and I just cannot picture this event without you. Looking forward to having you amidst us!

As we have decided to hold a party on [date], it would not be possible without you. You are cordially invited to my party and make the party convivial.

People like you are the charm of any party. And that's why we are looking forward to having you with us to make it rock and awesome. Don't be late!

Invitation messages for dinner

We invite you to join us on [date] as we have planned to throw a dinner party at our residence!

We are going to arrange a dinner party at our sweet home on [date]. Your presence is what we are asking for to make it a memorable one!

Sending you my heartiest invitation to join this dinner party. Your presence is all that's needed to make this party a memorable one.

You are most cordially invited to be our guest at the dinner party we have arranged on [date]. It will be great having you among us!

Your company is all that we are asking for as we celebrate the night of [date] with our friends and relatives. Please join us to have a share in our happiness!

We want to celebrate this night with some good food and good people. It'd be really appreciated if you could join us.

Invitation messages for graduation party

All the hard works he did for all these years have finally brought a reward so sweet. We want to celebrate his efforts by throwing a graduation party. You are invited!

We are joyfully inviting you to be a part of the graduation party in honor of our sweet [name] on [date]. Your presence means a lot for all of us.

Please join us at on [date] at the graduation party thrown in the name of [name] as he becomes a proud graduate on [subject].

Let us all share in the joy of [name] for becoming a fresh graduate. Your blessings will be an inspiration for his new journey. Cordially invite you to the party!

We are looking forward to celebrating the graduation party with many fond memories and a fantastic group of friends. We would be glad if you could spend some valuable time with us.

It is my humble request to attend the graduation party. I want to celebrate the successes with my near and dear ones. You're cordially invited.

Invitation messages for birthday party

At our boy's / girl's birthday party, we're hoping to have all the people whom he / she loves and adores. Your presence will be much appreciated.

We have made the arrangements for this birthday party, but it is your presence that will make this party grand! Do come.

The fun of any party relies on the presence of our loved ones. We are cordially inviting you to join our baby's birthday party.

Your attending the party is the best gift my baby could ask for his birthday. Please join us on this delightful occasion.

We're sending you the warmest invitation to join our child's birthday party. Please come and share the joy of this occasion with us.

Invitation messages for get-together party

You have always been an integral part of our lives. The evening of [date] will be of less joy if your presence is missed by all. You are invited!

Time may have changed our lives and divided our paths, but it couldn't erase the memories from our hearts. You are invited to the get-together party of [date].

You have always been the true star in our circle of friends. We all are eagerly waiting to have you with us on [date] as a get-together party has been announced!

It doesn't matter where we are and what we do, we can never ignore the place where our hearts truly belong. Please join us on the get-together party of [place].

Why not gather and whoop it up together? It has been a long time since we met. Let's meet over a get-together. We will be waiting for you!

Invitation messages for farewell party

A farewell party has been announced in honor of everyone's favorite Mr. / Mrs. [name] on [date]. You are cordially invited to be a part of the moment!

Let us all be together to celebrate the highly decorated professional life of Mr. / Mrs. [name] as he waves goodbye to us. You are invited!

He's been our truest friend and most ideal mentor in the profession. Let us take some time off on [date] to bid an unforgettable farewell to him.

Very few people can touch our hearts and make a permanent place in it. Our beloved [name] is surely one of them. We invite you to join us as we say goodbye to this amazing person!

We request your presence for the evening filled with memories and recounting interesting tales over drinks and dinner. Kindly come to the farewell party of [name, party venue, and date].

Invitation messages for office party

You're a deeply valued person in this office, and any of our gatherings would be empty without you. We invite you to join us on [date] at the office party!

Let us all celebrate the success of our company with wines and whiskey. Your presence there will add a great amount of joy for all.

An office party has been arranging on [date]. Your presence is required as your part there is no less important than the boss himself!

We have decided to take a day off, not to stay idle at home but to celebrate the success of our company by throwing an office party. You are invited!

You bring so much joy to this office, now we're hoping to see you do the same to this party. Do attend it!

Invitation messages for bachelor party

My days of singlehood are finally coming to an end. Time is running fast, don't miss the chance to celebrate my bachelor party on [date and time].

For brotherhood, for beers, and for the last singlehood moments! Come and rock my bachelor party! You are cordially invited, let's see you at [date, time and venue].

Guys! Our buddy is finally getting hitched. Let's paint the town as [name]'s single life is winding down. So what are you waiting for? Grab a beer, pick a suit and hop in.

In honor of our brother, [name], join us as we give the last hooray to his singlehood and his freedom. So tiptoe at [venue] on [date and time] sharp.

It's top-secret! We have sneakily slipped in a surprise bachelor party for our friend who is about to bid adieu to his single days. Join us [date and time] at [venue].

Let's have a blast and rock the stag night with music and drinks. You are invited to Freedom [name] Party! So come and party till your energy runs out!

Invitation messages for bachelorette party

Before the wedding, the bride deserves to have one last silly night. Let's join this party to give her that.

This is the last party we get before this Miss turns into a Mrs. Do join to make it a memorable one!

Before she ties the knot, let's give her one last taste of living the single life. Please attend the party!

Your presence will double the fun of this girls' night. For the sake of this would-be bride, let's party!

Let's celebrate the bride-to-be with the most joyous party ever! Join us to make this party a success.

(Adapted from *wishesmsg.com*)

Sources of Pictures

Pic. 5-1 Retrieved from *eslbuzz.com*
Pic. 5-2 Retrieved from *7esl.com*
Pic. 5-3 Retrieved from *englishan.com*
Pic. 5-4 Retrieved from *7esl.com*
Pic. 5-5 Retrieved from *7esl.com*

References

Robert Rich. (2020). Sports and Exercise at Every Age. *familydoctor.org*. Retrieved from https://familydoctor.org/sports-and-exercise-at-every-age/.

Joe Denton. (2021). Going to Sporting Events. *eventbrite Blog*. Retrieved from https://www.eventbrite.com/blog/ds00-5-reasons-people-go-to-sporting-events-and-what-we-can-learn-from-them/.

National Institute on Aging (NIA). (2020). Setting Fitness Goals. *U.S. Department of Health & Services*. Retrieved from https://www.nia.nih.gov/health/how-older-adults-can-get-started-exercise#fitnessgoals.

Five Misconceptions about Exercise. *Habits of Health*. Retrieved from https://www.habitsofhealth.com/2019/05/5-misconceptions-about-exercise/on July 9, 2021.

Joining a Gym. *British Council*. Retrieved from https://learnenglish.britishcouncil.org/skills/listening/upper-intermediate-b2/joining-a-gym on July 9, 2021.

Brendon Rearick. (2021). Working out at a Gym. *wikiHow*. Retrieved from https://www.wikihow.com/Get-Fit-in-the-Gym.

Alice. E. M. Underwood. (2017). All the Sports Words Only Americans Use.

grammarly blog. Retrieved from https://www.grammarly.com/blog/sports-words/.

Georgia Taylor. Learning and Living Overseas. *MDPI*. Retrieved from https://www.mdpi.com/2227—7102/7/1/35/htm on July 9, 2021.

British Pub Culture. *GBMag*. Retrieved from https://greatbritishmag. co. uk/uk-culture/british-pub-culture/on July 9, 2021.

Chris Macleod. What Do People Actually Do at Parties? *Succeed Socially*. Retrieved from https://www.succeedsocially.com/whathappensatparties on July 9, 2021.

Jennifer Landis. (2021). Attending a Dinner Party. *Millennial*. Retrieved from https://millennialmagazine.com/2021/07/08/tips-for-hosting-a-dinner-party-at-your-home/.

Natasha Miller. (2021). Throwing a Surprise Party. *wikiHow*. Retrieved from https://www.wikihow.com/Throw-a-Surprise-Party.

Alyssa Abel. (2021). How to Adjust as an International Student in America. *Niche*. Retrieved from https://www. niche. com/blog/how-to-adjust-as-an-international-student-in-america/.

Arlin Cuncic. (2020). How to Deal with Social Anxiety at a Party. *verywell mind*. Retrieved from https://www. verywellmind. com/how-to-deal-with-social-anxiety-at-a-party-3024417.

Party Invitation Messages. *WishesMsg.com*. Retrieved from https://www.*wishesmsg*.com/party-invitation-messages/on July 9, 2021.

Make Your Farewell Party a Memorable Event. *Party Joys*. Retrieved from https://partyjoys.com/farewell-party-ideas.